# MO
# HONEY IN THE
# KITCHEN

## Joyce White
## Revised by Valerie Rogers

Northern Bee Books

ISBN 978-1-904846-58-1


This edition, a reprint of the updated edition of
2001 is published in 2010 by

Northern Bee Books
Scout Bottom Farm
Mytholmroyd
Hebden Bridge HX7 5JS (UK)

Printed by in the United Kingdom by
Lightning Source UK Ltd., Milton Keynes

# Contents

Introduction and Acknowledgements iv

Oven Temperatures v

Average composition of honey vi

Cakes 1

Biscuits and Cookies 8

Meat dishes 13

Fish 25

Yeast and Bread 26

Puddings and Desserts 30

Preserves 48

Soup, Salads and Vegetables 50

Drinks 54

Sweets and Confectionery 55

Beeswax and other Bee products 59

Mead 61

Some recipes from the past 63

Index of Recipes 64

# Introduction to Revised edition and Acknowledgements

It has been a great privilege to revise *Honey in the Kitchen* and *More Honey in the Kitchen* in memory of my mother, a well known beekeeper and craftswoman. The grandchildren, now grown up, have opted to keep the drawings unchanged. Some of my own favourite honey recipes have been added, as well as a few kindly donated by others, notably Jane Jones and John and Jacy Kinross.

As I am not (yet!) a beekeeper I rely on purchased honey for my cooking, and I recommend to other non-beekeepers that you use the best flavoured honey that you can afford for the cakes and desserts, but that a cheaper 'supermarket' honey will be fine for those recipes which are more highly spiced, or which contain other strong flavours such as garlic.

Valerie Rogers
Fordingbridge
June, 2001

Cover photograph on this edition by John Phipps, cover design D&P Design and Print © 2010

# Average Composition of Honey

*100 g Honey contains the following:*

| | | |
|---|---|---|
| Water | 17.2 g | |
| Fructose | 38.2 g | |
| Glucose | 31.3 g | |
| Sucrose | 1.3 g | |
| Other sugars | 8.8 g | |
| Potassium | 10 mg | |
| Sodium | 5 mg | |
| Calcium | 5 mg | |
| Magnesium | 6 mg | |
| Iron | 0.5 mg | |
| Copper | 0.2 mg | |
| Manganese | 0.2 mg | |
| Phosphate | 16.0 mg | |
| Sulphate | 5.0 mg | |

Trace amounts of nicotinic acid, pantothenic acid, pyridoxin, riboflavin, thiamin, biotin, folic acid, ascorbic acid, several enzymes, traces of lipids and many other substances.

*To use honey in cooking.*—Honey is easier to measure in a spoon if the spoon is warmed.

*To weigh honey.*—Place the jar on the scales and take out honey until the weight is reduced by the required amount.

Imperial quantities are given first with metric in brackets. Use one or the other as the amounts are not exactly the same.

# Oven Temperatures

Note. For fan ovens, temperatures may be reduced. Refer to manufacturers' instructions.

| Heat of oven | Gas thermostat settings | Electric oven temperatures °F | °C |
|---|---|---|---|
| very cool | ¼ | 225 | 110 |
| "    " | ½ | 250 | 120 |
| cool | 1 | 275 | 140 |
| " | 2 | 300 | 150 |
| moderate | 3 | 325 | 160 |
| " | 4 | 350 | 180 |
| fairly hot | 5 | 375 | 190 |
| "    " | 6 | 400 | 200 |
| hot | 7 | 425 | 220 |
| very hot | 8 | 450 | 230 |
| "    " | 9 | 475 | 240 |

# CAKES

Several of Joyce's recipes use angelica. This is no longer a supermarket 'buy', but can be found in specialist shops. If not, it can be omitted.

## FAMILY CAKE

2 level tbsp (30 ml) honey
6 oz (150 g) margarine
12 oz (300 g) plain flour
2 level tsp (10 ml) mixed spice
4 oz (100 g) Demerara Sugar
8 oz (200 g) candied peel, cherries and angelica (chopped and mixed)
8 oz (200 g) grated carrot
1 medium sized apple
2 large eggs
1 level tsp (5 ml) bicarbonate of soda
2 tbsp (30 ml) milk

*Topping*
4 oz (100 g) almond paste or marzipan
6 glace cherries halved

Grease and line a 7″–8″ (18 cm–20 cm) round cake tin. Warm margarine and honey until melted. Sift flour and spice into mixing bowl. Stir in sugar, peel, cherries, angelica, carrot, beaten eggs and melted margarine and honey and grated apple. Mix well.

Dissolve the soda in the milk and stir into the mixture. Put in the tin.

Roll out the almond paste on a board sprinkled with icing sugar and cut into half inch wide strips. Arrange them lattice fashion on top of the cake. Lightly press a cherry into the spaces.

Bake in a pre-heated oven at 180°C (350°F, gas 4) for about $1^3/_4$ hours or until cooked. If the top starts to brown cover with a layer of greaseproof paper. Leave cake to cool in the tin.

## GINGER CAKE

4 oz (100 g) butter or margarine
2 oz (50 g) soft brown sugar
2 oz (50 g) honey

1 beaten egg
4 oz (100 g) self-raising flour
1 heaped tsp (8 ml) baking powder
6 fl oz (175 ml) milk
2 oz (50 g) oatmeal
½ oz (15 g) crystallised ginger (chopped) or sultanas
1 dsp (10 ml) ground ginger
1½ tbsp (20 ml) lemon juice
1 tbsp (15 ml) honey

Cream the fat, sugar and honey and beat in the egg.

Sieve the dry ingredients and add with the crystallised ginger or sultanas, then add the milk and oats. Mix well.

Pour into a greased and lined tin. Bake at 180°C (350°F, gas 4) for about 60 minutes.

Blend the honey and lemon juice and pour over the cake while still warm.

## HONEY MARMALADE CAKE

4 oz (100 g) margarine
4 oz (100 g) sugar
2 eggs
10 oz (250 g) plain flour
2 level teasps. (10 ml) baking powder
3 oz (75 g) honey
4 oz (100 g) marmalade

Cream the fat and sugar, beat the eggs and add gradually, slightly warm the honey and marmalade and stir into the mixture with the flour and sifted baking powder. Place in a greased and lined 7 inch (18 cm) tin and bake in a slow oven for 1 to 1¼ hours at 150°C (300°F, gas 2) until firm and golden brown.

## HONEY CAKE

4 oz (100 g) butter or margarine
6 oz (150 g) honey
8 oz (200 g) self-raising flour
6 oz (150 g) sultanas
2 eggs

Cream the fat and honey, beat the eggs well and add with sifted flour. Beat well and lightly. A little milk may be added if necessary. Turn in sultanas and mix well. Bake in a round tin 6½″–7½″ diameter for about 1¼ hours in a moderate oven.

This recipe is especially included as it is suitable for Honey Shows.

## SPICED APPLE CAKE

12 oz (300 g) self-raising flour
2 tsp (10 ml) mixed spice
6 oz (175 g) margarine
4 oz (100 g) soft brown sugar
2 oz (50 g) honey
8 oz (200 g) sultanas
8 fl oz (200 ml) milk
1 beaten egg
8 oz (200 g) cooking apples (peeled and sliced)
1 oz (25 g) Demerara Sugar
1 dsp (10 ml) honey to glaze

Mix flour with spices. Rub in the fat, add the sugar and sultanas. Warm honey slightly and blend with the milk and egg. Add to the dry ingredients and mix well.

Place half the mixture into a greased loaf or cake tin, cover with half the apple slices. Spread the rest of the cake mixture on the apples and spread the remaining apples over the top. Warm the honey and spread over the apples. Sprinkle the Demerara on top.

Bake at 170°C (330°F, gas 3) until well risen and golden brown (about 1½ hours).

## JOYCE'S DATE AND GINGER CAKE

10 oz (250 g) plain flour
6 oz (150 g) soft margarine
2 oz (50 g) soft brown sugar
1 tsp (5 ml) bicarbonate of soda
3 tsp (15 ml) powdered ginger
2 tsp (10 ml) powdered cinnamon
2 eggs—beaten
4 oz (100 g) honey
5 fl oz (125 ml) milk
2–3 pieces stem ginger in syrup
4 oz (100g) chopped dates

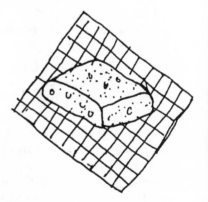

Melt the margarine and honey together and allow to cool. Beat the eggs into the milk. Sift the flour, bicarbonate of soda and spices together and chop the ginger.

Mix the wet ingredients into the dry and add the fruit. Pour the batter into a greased and lined cake tin, 8" × 10" (20 cm × 25 cm) and bake in the oven at 170°C (330°F, gas 3). Remove from the oven when cooked and brush with the ginger syrup before cutting into pieces. This recipe was a great mainstay in Joyce's kitchen.

## HONEY TEA BREAD

**8 oz (200 g) self-raising flour**
**½ tsp (2.5 ml) mixed spice**
**4 oz (100 g) margarine**
**2 oz (50 g) soft brown sugar**
**3 oz (75 g) honey**
**6 oz (150 g) mixed dried fruit**
**2 eggs**
**honey to glaze**

Grease and line a loaf tin, 9" × 5" (23 cm × 13 cm). Sieve the flour and spice together in a bowl, rub in the margarine. Stir in the sugar, fruit, eggs (beaten) and honey. Mix well.

Bake in tin, 1–1¼ hours at 180°C (350°F, gas 4), cover top with cooking foil halfway through cooking if it is getting too brown. Cook until firm. Cool slightly on rack and brush with honey. Serve sliced and buttered for tea.

## COCONUT COOKIES

**4 oz (100 g) butter**
**3½ oz (85 g) soft brown sugar**
**3 oz (75 g) desiccated coconut**
**3 oz (75 g) rolled oats**
**6 tbsp cornflakes**
**1 tbsp (15 ml) honey**

Grease a shallow square or rectangular cake tin. Mix sugar, coconut, rolled oats and cornflakes. Warm butter and honey, stirring. Remove from heat and stir into dry ingredients. Spread into the cake tin and bake for about 30 minutes at 160°C (350°F, gas 3) until golden brown.

Cut into squares and leave to cool in the tin.

## PARKIN

8 oz (200 g) plain flour
8 oz (200 g) oatmeal
6 oz (150 g) margarine
6 oz (150 g) sugar
1 tsp (5 ml) bicarbonate of soda
2 tbsp (30 ml) honey
5 fl oz (125 ml) milk
1 dsp (10 ml) ginger

Sieve the flour, ginger, sugar and bicarbonate into a bowl. Melt the fat with the honey and add to the flour mixture with the milk and oatmeal. Mix all well together and pour into a well greased baking tin. Cook at 150°C (300°F, gas 2) for 50–60 minutes. Cut into squares while still warm.

## SEEDY CAKE

8 oz (200 g) self-raising flour
4 oz (100 g) butter or margarine
3 oz (75 g) soft brown sugar
1 tbsp (15 ml) honey
1 tbsp (20 g) caraway seeds
2 small eggs (or 1 large egg)
4 fl oz (100 ml) milk

Sift the flour, rub in the margarine lightly and add the sugar and caraway seeds. Beat the egg and mix it with the milk. Add to the dry ingredients and fold in well. Bake in a lined tin, 7″ (18 cm), for about 1–1¼ hours at 160°C (325°F, gas 3).

## HONEY SPONGE

6 oz (150 g) butter or margarine
4 oz (100 g) caster sugar
1 tbsp (15 ml) honey
6 oz (150 g) self-raising flour
3 eggs
about 2 tbsp (40 ml) warm water

Cream the margarine with the honey and sugar until light and fluffy. Gradually add the beaten eggs and mix in well. Carefully fold in the sifted flour and add a little water, if required, to make a soft mixture.

Grease and line two 7″ (18 cm) sandwich tins. Divide the mixture between the two tins and smooth the tops. Bake in the centre of a moderate oven (180°C, (350°F, gas 4)) until golden and springy to the touch.

Cool on a wire rack.


## COFFEE RUM FILLING

6 oz (150 g) unsalted butter or hard margarine
2 oz (50 g) brown sugar
2 oz (50 g) honey } or 4 oz (100 g) honey
4 tsp (20 ml) instant coffee dissolved in 1–2 tbsp (15–30 ml)
  boiling water
1 tbsp (15 ml) rum

Beat all ingredients to a smooth paste and use to sandwich together the honey sponge. Any surplus can be stored in a covered container in a refrigerator until required.


## YOGHURT AND RASPBERRY FILLING

1 small carton yoghurt (plain)
1 punnet raspberries (or strawberries)
1 tsp (5 ml) honey
a little icing sugar

Spread the bottom layer of the sponge with yoghurt. Arrange the fruit on this. Slightly warm the honey to make it run and dribble over the fruit. Before putting the top of the sponge on, cut it into wedges without cutting right through. Lift carefully on to the top of the cake (this enables the cake to be cut without squashing out the fruit and yoghurt). Sprinkle a little icing sugar on the top.


## SOFT WHITE FROSTING FOR CAKES (will cover 8″ (20 cm) round cake)

1 egg white
6 oz (150 g) caster sugar
1 dsp (10 ml) honey
3 tbsp (45 ml) water
½ tsp (2.5 ml) vanilla essence
a pinch of salt

Put all ingredients except vanilla in a bowl standing in a pan of boiling water. Beat for about 6–8 minutes with a hand or electric mixer until the mixture is thickened and will stand up in peaks. Add vanilla essence and beat for another five minutes.

Spread over the top of the cake with a palette knife.


## ORANGE LOAF

2 oz (50 g) margarine
10 oz (250 g) honey
9 oz (225 g) self-raising flour
1 large egg
grated rind of 1 orange
juice of 1 large orange

Cream honey and fat, add the beaten egg and orange rind and mix in. Sift the flour and add alternately with the orange juice.

Put into a greased loaf tin and bake at 160°C (300°F, gas 2) for about one hour.


## GILLIE'S HONEY CAKE

5 oz (125 g) butter
4 oz (100 g) soft brown sugar
6 oz (150 g) clear honey
1 tabsp water
2 eggs
7 oz (200 g) wholewheat self-raising flour
Flaked almonds to decorate

Measure butter, sugar, honey and water into a saucepan. Place over low heat till blended. Remove and cool. Beat in eggs thoroughly one by one. Add all flour at once till smooth.

Pour into greased tin, sprinkle with the almonds and bake in a moderate oven 160°C (325°F, gas 3).

# BISCUITS AND COOKIES

## OAT COOKIES

4 oz (100 g) margarine
2 oz (50 g) soft brown sugar
2 oz (50 g) honey
1 egg
8 oz (200 g) porridge oats
1 tsp (5 ml) baking powder

Cream together the margarine, sugar, and honey until light. Stir in the beaten egg, oats and baking powder.

Turn onto a floured board and knead lightly until well mixed. Roll out thinly and cut into rounds.

Place on a greased baking tray and cook for 15–20 minutes until golden at 170°C (325°F, gas 3). These can be eaten as biscuits or spread with butter and eaten with cheese.

## RAISIN AND OAT BISCUITS

6 oz (175 g) caster sugar
3 tablespoons (45 ml) honey
6 oz (175 g) margarine
2 egg whites
½ teaspoon (2.5 ml) grated orange peel
8 oz (200 g) porridge oats
4 oz (100 g) self-raising flour
3 oz (75 g) raisins

Beat the sugar, honey and margarine until light and fluffy. Add the orange peel and egg whites. Mix well.

Combine the flour and oats and gently add to the mixture with the raisins. Lightly grease a swiss roll tin and bake at 180°C (350°F, gas 4) for about 15 minutes, until golden.

Cut into slices or wedges in the tin. Remove from the tin when cool.

## FLAPJACKS

5 oz (125 g) margarine or butter
3 oz (75 g) light brown sugar

3 oz (75 g) honey
8 oz (200 g) porridge oats

Melt the fat, sugar and honey in a pan. Mix in the oats and stir well.

Press into an 8″ (20 cm) square tin and smooth the surface with the back of a spoon.

Bake at 180°C (350°F, gas 4) for 25–30 minutes—until set and golden brown. Mark into slices or squares while still warm and leave to cool on a wire tray.


## FRUITY FLAPJACKS

6 oz (150 g) margarine or butter
4 oz (100 g) light brown sugar
1 tbsp (15 ml) honey
8 oz (200 g) porridge oats
6 oz (150 g) dried fruit

Melt the fat, honey and sugar in a bowl or pan.

Stir in the porridge oats and mix well. Add the fruit and stir in. Grease a baking tin 11″ × 7″ or 30 cm × 20 cm.

Press the mixture into the tin and bake at 180°C (350°F, gas 4) for about 20 minutes, until golden brown.

Cut into fingers while warm and leave to cool before removing from the tin.

The flavour can be varied:

Add orange and lemon peel, grated or candied, cherries, walnuts, etc.


## HONEY NUT BISCUITS

4 oz (100 g) margarine
4 oz (100 g) light brown sugar
1 beaten egg
1 tablespoon (15 ml) honey
8 oz (200 g) self-raising flour
2 oz (50 g) chopped nuts

Cream the fat and sugar and beat in the egg and honey.

Sift the flour and beat into the mixture, add nuts and mix to a soft dough.

Form into small balls with the hands.

Place on greased baking sheets, well apart and slightly flattened with a damp fork.

Bake at 180°C (350°F, gas 4) for about 15 minutes—until golden brown. Allow to cool, then transfer to a wire rack.

## OATY FRUIT BISCUITS

6 oz (175 g) butter or margarine
1 egg
3 oz (75 g) dark brown sugar
2 oz (50 g) honey
2 oz (50 g) raisins, cherries or sultanas (or a mixture of these)
10 oz (250 g) self-raising flour (white or brown)
2–3 oz (50–75 g) rolled oats for cooking

Cream the fat and sugar and beat in the egg, honey and milk. Fold in the flour (it should make a fairly stiff dough). Form into balls (about 24 to 28). Place on a greased baking tray with room to spread.
  Bake at 180°C (350°F, gas 4) for 15–20 minutes until golden.
  Cool on a wire rack.


## FAIRING BISCUITS

4 oz (100 g) plain flour
¼ tsp (1 ml) ground ginger
¼ tsp (1 ml) mixed spice
¼ tsp (1 ml) cinnamon
1½ tsp (7 ml) bicarbonate of soda
2 oz (50 g) butter or margarine
2 oz (50 g) sugar
2 oz (50 g) honey

Mix the flour, ginger, spice, cinnamon and bicarbonate of soda in a bowl. Add butter or margarine and mix or process until it looks like breadcrumbs. Add the sugar and honey and beat until smooth. Put the mixture in teaspoonfuls about 2 inches (5 cm) apart on a greased baking tray. Bake at 180°C (350°F, gas 4) for 10 minutes. Take the tray from the oven and tap it on a hard surface to spread the biscuits and return to the oven for a further 5 minutes or until firm.


## HONEY AND OATMEAL BISCUITS

4 oz (100 g) plain flour
4 oz (100 g) margarine or butter
3 oz (75 g) sugar—white or soft brown
4 oz (100 g) porridge oats
1 dsp (10 ml) honey
a few drops of vanilla essence

*EITHER* cream the fat, sugar, honey and essence and stir in the dry ingredients. Mix well.
*OR* put all the ingredients into a food processor and blend until mixed. Roll out and cut to shape. Arrange on a lightly greased baking tray.

Bake at 180°C (350°F, gas 4) for 10–15 minutes until golden. Cool on a wire rack. Serve plain or with cheese.

## HONEY GINGER BISCUITS

**8 oz (200 g) self-raising flour**
**1 heaped tsp (10 ml) ground ginger**
**3 oz (75 g) sugar—soft brown**
**3 oz (75 g) margarine**
**3 oz (75 g) honey**
**1 egg**

Mix the flour, sugar and ginger. Warm the honey and margarine and beat together. Beat the egg. Add the flour mixture and egg, a little at a time, to the honey mixture. Mix well. Roll out on a floured board and cut into shapes. Place on a greased baking tray and cook at 180°C (350°F, gas 4) for 12–15 minutes until golden.

Cool on a wire rack.

## BOURBON CREAM BISCUITS

*Biscuits*
**2 oz (50 g) butter or margarine**
**2 oz (50 g) muscavado sugar**
**1 tbsp (15 ml) honey**
**4 oz (100 g) plain flour**
**2 tbsp (30 ml) cocoa powder**
**½ tsp (2.5 ml) bicarbonate of soda**

*Filling*
**1½ oz (37 g) margarine**
**3 oz (75 g) icing sugar**
**1 tsp (5 ml) coffee essence**
**1 tbsp (15 ml) cocoa powder**

Cream the fat and sugar. Add the honey, sieved flour, cocoa and bicarbonate to the mixture. Mix to a stiff dough. Roll out to 3mm thick. Cut into fingers 6.5 cm × 1.5 cm. Prick with a fork.

Place on a greased baking tray. Bake at 170°C (325°F, gas 3) for 15–20 minutes. Put on a wire rack to cool.

*Filling*

Cream margarine and icing sugar, add coffee and cocoa and mix until creamy. Sandwich the fingers together with the filling.

Store in an airtight tin.


## GOLDEN CRUNCH BISCUITS

3 oz (75 g) plain flour
½ tsp (2.5 ml) baking powder
3 oz (75 g) Demerara or soft brown sugar
3 oz (75 g) porridge oats
3 oz (75 g) butter or margarine
1 tbsp (15 ml) honey
½ tsp (2.5 ml) bicarbonate of soda
1 tbsp (15 ml) milk

Sift flour and baking powder into a bowl, add sugar and oats and mix well. Warm the margarine with the honey and mix. Mix the milk with the bicarbonate of soda. Add all together and mix well.

Place small balls of mixture well apart on a lightly greased baking tray. Bake at 180°C (350°F, gas 4) for about 10 minutes until flat and golden.

Leave to cool before transferring to a wire rack.


## FRUIT AND GINGER BISCUITS

4 oz (100 g) plain flour
2 oz (50 g) margarine or butter
2 oz (50 g) soft brown sugar
1½ tbsp (20 ml) honey
½ tsp (2.5 ml) ground ginger
1 tbsp (15 ml) chopped mixed peel
1 tbsp (15 ml) chopped nuts

Mix the flour and sugar in a bowl, warm margarine and honey until soft and add to flour with ginger and beat until smooth. Add peel and nuts and mix in.

Take out teaspoons of mixture and form into balls. Placed on a greased baking tray and flatten a little. Allow a little space for them to expand. Cook at 170°C (325°F, gas 3) for 10–15 minutes until golden brown. Remove from trays while still warm and cool on a wire rack.

# MEAT DISHES

## BARBECUED SPARE RIBS

2 lb (900 g) spare ribs of pork
2 tbsp (30 ml) tomato puree
4 tbsp (60 ml) soy sauce
2 tbsp (30 ml) honey
2 cloves of garlic—crushed
1 onion—grated
2 tsp (10 ml) mustard

Separate the spare ribs and spread in a large dish. Mix all the other ingredients and brush over the meat. Cook for 45 minutes at 180°C (350°F, gas 4).

Turn the meat over and baste, then cook for a further 15 minutes until well browned and tender. Serve hot.


## GLAZED PORK CHOPS WITH ORANGE

4 pork chops or cutlets
oil for frying
4 slices apple
4 slices orange
1 dsp (10 ml) gravy powder or 1 stock cube
1½ dsp (15ml) honey
15 fl oz (375 ml) water
1 dsp (10 ml) cornflour
salt & pepper to season

Heat the oil in a pan and brown the meat on both sides. Pour off excess oil and any fat. Place an apple and orange slice on each chop and hold in place with cocktail sticks. Make up stock with the gravy powder, water and seasoning. Pour over the chops. Dribble the honey on to the fruit, cover the pan and simmer for 30–40 minutes, or until tender. Place on a warmed dish. Mix the cornflour and orange juice, add to the pan and simmer for a few minutes, stirring. Pour over the chops or serve separately in a gravy jug.

## HONEY GLAZED PORK CHOPS OR FILLETS

2 pork loin chops or fillets
salt and freshly ground pepper
1 tbsp (15 ml) honey
5 tbsp (75 ml) dry cider
1 tsp (5 ml) sage—chopped
1 tbsp (15 ml) cooking oil

Season pork with salt and pepper. Heat the oil in a pan, add the pork and brown on both sides. Mix the honey with the sage and cider. Pour over the meat and cook in the oven at 200°C (400°F, gas 6) until tender—about 40 minutes. Turn the chops over halfway through the cooking time. Serve the meat with the sauce poured over it.

## SWEET AND SOUR PORK BALLS

12 oz (350 mg) minced raw pork or ham
1 onion (peeled and chopped)
1 tbsp (15 ml) cooking oil
½ a red pepper ⎫
½ a green pepper ⎬ or red pepper sliced and seeded
½ a yellow pepper ⎭
1 tbsp (15 ml) red wine vinegar
1 tbsp (15 ml) honey
1 tsp (5 ml) soy sauce
5 tbsp (75 ml) unsweetened orange juice
5 tbsp (75 ml) stock—chicken or pork
a pinch of ground ginger
a pinch of spice
salt and pepper
2 tsp (10 ml) cornflour

Mix pork, onion, salt and pepper, blending well. Shape into small balls.

Heat the oil in a pan. Add the meat balls and cook until browned all over. Remove with a straining spoon, place on a warmed dish and keep warm. Add the peppers to the pan and cook until soft. Add the rest of the ingredients, except the cornflour, and cook until tender.

Add the cornflour, mixed to a smooth paste with a little water. Bring to simmering point for ½ a minute, then pour over the pork balls.

## HONEY GLAZED HAM

1 ham joint (gammon, corner, etc)
1 tbsp (15 ml) honey
a few cloves
1 tsp (5 ml) mustard powder
¼ pint (125 ml) unsweetened orange juice

Put the ham in a pan, cover it with water and bring to the boil. Pour off the water. Return the pan to the hob add more water to come halfway up the joint. Simmer for 1–1½ hours or until tender.

Drain off the water and cut the skin off the meat. Score the fat into diamonds and brush over the honey, mustard and orange juice mixed to a paste. Push a few cloves into the meat where the scoring lines cross. Put the ham into a casserole and bake in the oven at 200°C (400°F, gas 6) for about 30 minutes. Serve hot or cold.


## HONEY GLAZED BACON WITH STUFFED APPLES

3 lb (1½ kg) joint of gammon bacon
6 small cooking apples
3 oz (75 g) breadcrumbs
1 small onion
1 stick of celery
a few cloves
a few sage leaves
1 small egg
2 tbs (30 ml) honey
1 tbs (15 ml) chopped fresh parsley
1 tsp dried sage

Put the bacon in a saucepan, cover with water and bring to boiling. Remove with a spoon any scum that rises to the surface. Cover and let it simmer for an hour.

Drain off the water and lay the bacon in a roasting tin or oven dish. Cover with a lid or foil for 30 minutes in the oven at 180°C (350°F, gas 4).

Chop the onion and celery, mix in a bowl with the parsley, dried sage, breadcrumbs and a little salt and pepper. Bind together with the beaten egg.

Remove the cores from the apples and score them round the centres to prevent bursting. Stuff them firmly with the mixture.

Remove the fat from the meat and score the fat with a knife in a diamond pattern. Push in cloves where the score lines cross and brush over with the honey. Put the stuffed apples round the meat and return to the oven. Cook for about half an hour or until the meat is tender. Garnish with the sage leaves.

## BACON SLICES WITH PINEAPPLE AND GINGER

2 slices of gammon bacon or bacon chops
1 small tin of unsweetened pineapple
2 tbsp (30 ml) dry white wine
2 tsp (10 ml) lemon juice
1 tbsp (15 ml) honey
1½ tsp (8 ml) Worcester sauce
1 tsp (5 ml) cornflour
1 tsp (5 ml) ground ginger

Snip the bacon fat to prevent it from curling and place in a shallow dish with a lid. Mix pineapple juice, honey, lemon, ginger, wine, sauce and cornflour. Pour over the chops and cook with the lid on at 180°C (350°F, gas 4) for 30–40 minutes, turning over halfway. When tender, arrange pineapple slices on top of the meat.

Serve hot with vegetables.


## LAMB AND APPLE STEW

1 lb (450 g) boneless lamb—cut into cubes and fat removed
1 medium sized onion
¼ pint (125 ml) water with
½ a stock cube (or gravy granules)
salt and pepper
1 large cooking apple
1 tbsp (15 ml) honey
¼ tsp ground cinnamon
a pinch of mixed spice
a little grated orange rind
sunflower or soya oil for frying

Heat the oil in a pan and gently fry the onion until clear and soft. Transfer to a casserole. Add meat to the pan and brown over moderate heat. Add to the onions.

Bring stock to simmering point, add to the meat and season with salt and pepper. Put the lid on the casserole and bake in a slow oven 160°C (325°F, gas 3) for 1–1½ hours.

Peel and core the apple and cut into slices. Add to the casserole with honey and spices. Cook for ³/₄ to 1 hour until the apples are soft.

Serve hot with vegetables.

## LAMB STEAKS

4 lamb leg steaks
1 tbsp (15 ml) oil (sunflower or soya)
1 medium sized onion
1 tsp (5 ml) powdered ginger
2 tbsp (30 ml) dry, red wine
½ pint lamb or vegetable stock
a few redcurrants
1 tbsp (15 ml) honey
salt and pepper
1 tbsp (15 ml) chopped fresh mint

Heat the oil in a pan. Cook the lamb on both sides until cooked and tender. Remove from pan and keep warm. Fry onion, add ginger and stir-fry for 1 minute. Add stock, wine, redcurrants and honey, bring to simmering point and simmer for 3–5 minutes. Spoon some of the sauce over the lamb and serve the rest in a gravy dish.

## LEG OF LAMB

1 leg of lamb about 3–4 lb
1 tbsp (15 ml) honey
½ oz butter or margarine
1 dsp (10 ml) redcurrant jelly
a pinch of cinnamon
salt and pepper
1 tbsp (15 ml) tomato ketchup

Bone the meat joint and, with a sharp knife, cut it to make a flat joint. Season meat with pepper and cook in the oven at 190°C (375°F, gas 5) for 20 minutes.

Mix the rest of the ingredients and cook in a small pan for 3–4 minutes. Remove the lamb from the oven and pour off the fat. Spoon half the sauce over the top of the meat. Cook for 10 minutes. Pour the rest of the sauce over it and cook for another 45 minutes. Cover with a lid or foil and leave for 10 minutes.

Carve the meat into thin slices and serve with the sauce spooned on top.

## STUFFED BREAST OF LAMB

1–1½ lb (600 g) breast of lamb (boned)
1 medium sized onion
8 oz (200 g) cooking apples
1 dsp (10 ml) honey
3 oz (75 g) breadcrumbs
¼ tsp (1.25 g) ground cloves
1 oz (25 g) sultanas or raisins
2 tsp (10 ml) chopped rosemary leaves
3 tbsp (45 ml) mead or cider
salt and pepper to season

Chop onion and cook until clear and tender in a pan or microwave. Add all the other ingredients (except the lamb) to the onion and mix well adding enough of the liquid to bind it together.

Lay the lamb flat and cut off excess fat. Spread the stuffing over the meat, then roll it up and tie with string in several places.

Place in a meat tin or glass cooking dish and cover with a lid or cooking foil. Roast for 1¼–1½ hours at 180°C (350°F, gas 4) until the lamb feels tender and is browned on the outside.

Make a gravy with the cooking juices and serve cut in slices with vegetables.


## GLAZED CORNED BEEF

1 tin (1 lb) corned beef
5 oz (125 g) marmalade (Seville orange or lemon)
a pinch of dry ginger powder
4 fl oz (100 ml) orange juice
pepper
1 tbsp (15 ml) honey

Cut the corned beef into slices and lay in an overproof dish. Put the marmalade, ginger, orange juice, pepper and honey into a small pan and gently cook for 3–4 minutes.

Pour the sauce over the corned beef and cook for approximately 20 minutes at 180°C (350°F, gas 4) until the corned beef is heated and the sauce has glazed the top.

Serve hot with vegetables or salad.

# FILLET STEAK WITH HONEY AND YOGHURT SAUCE

1 lb (450 g) fillet steak
salt and freshly ground black pepper
1 dsp (10 ml) cooking oil or beef dripping
1 tsp (5 ml) honey
4 tbsp (60 ml) yoghurt
2 tsp (10 ml) green peppercorns

Season steak with salt and pepper. Heat the oil or fat in a pan, add the steak and brown evenly on both sides. Reduce heat and cook until tender. Remove the steak from the pan and cut into slices. Place on a warmed serving dish.

Add the yoghurt, honey and peppercorns to the pan and blend well with the juices. Heat and simmer for a minute, then spoon over the steak and serve.


# BEEF WITH GINGER

1 lb (450 g) braising steak
2 oz (50 g) wholemeal flour
1 ½ tsp (7 ml) ground ginger
2 tbsp (30 ml) cooking oil
1 dsp (10 ml) grated root ginger
1 small clove of garlic—chopped
1 onion—chopped
½ pint (250 ml) beef stock (or water with gravy granules)
8 oz (200 g) tin of tomatoes
1 dsp (10 ml) vinegar
1 tbsp (15 ml) honey
1 tbsp (15 ml) Worcester sauce
1 15 oz (450 g) tin of red kidney beans
salt and freshly ground black pepper

Trim the meat and cut into cubes. Coat them with flour seasoned with salt, pepper and ground ginger. Heat the oil in a pan and fry the meat, turning several times to seal it. Place in a casserole.

Fry the root ginger, garlic and onion in the same pan, then add the remaining flour and cook for a minute. Gradually add all the other ingredients except beans, with salt and pepper to taste. Pour over the beef.

Cover the casserole and cook in a pre-heated oven, 160°C (350°F, gas 3) for about 1³/₄–2 hours until tender. Heat the beans and strain and add. Cook for a further 10 mins.

## SAUSAGES WITH BARBECUE SAUCE

1 lb (450 g) sausages (pork, beef etc)
1 oz (25 g) cooking fat or oil
1 small onion—finely chopped
1 clove of garlic—crushed
6 oz (175 g) tomatoes—skinned and
  chopped *or* tinned tomatoes
2 tbsp (30 ml) honey
1 tbsp (15 ml) tomato puree
2 tbsp (30 ml) soy sauce
1 tbsp (15 ml) vinegar
1 tbsp (15 ml) Worcester sauce
parsley or watercress to garnish

Warm the oil in a pan, add the onion and garlic and cook gently until clear and soft. Add tomatoes, stir in and cook until soft. Add the other ingredients, bring to the boiling point and simmer gently for 10 minutes.

Separate the sausages, brush a little sauce over them and cook either under the grill, turning frequently, or in the oven. Brush with more sauce when they are turned over.

When cooked, arrange in a dish, pour the rest of the hot sauce over them, then serve with vegetables, bread or rolls etc.

This sauce could also be used with beefburgers, chicken drumsticks etc.


## LAMB WITH LEMON AND HONEY

2 lb (1 kg) lamb—leg cut etc
1 medium onion
1 clove of garlic
juice of half a lemon
1 tbsp (15 ml) honey
1 tbsp (15 ml) soy or mint sauce

Put the meat in a baking dish and cook at 190°C (375°F, gas 5) for 10 minutes.

Chop onions, crush garlic and mix with other ingredients. Drain the fat from the meat, turn it over and pour the sauce on top. Lower the oven temperature to 180°C (350°F, gas 4) and cook for 1 hour, basting at intervals.

Cut into slices and serve with the sauce on top.

## HORSERADISH SAUCE (to serve with beef)

2 tbsp (30 ml) grated horseradish
1 tbsp (15 ml) white vinegar
½ tsp (2.5 ml) dry mustard
1 tsp (5 ml) honey
salt and pepper
5 fl oz (125 ml) cream—whipped

Mix together the horseradish, honey and mustard. Fold into the whipped cream. Add the vinegar, salt and pepper, mix well.


## APPLE SAUCE (to serve with pork)

½ lb cooking apples—cored and sliced
a little lemon juice
1 tsp (5 ml) honey
2 tsp (10 ml) water

Place all the ingredients into a covered bowl and microwave on HIGH for 4 – 5 minutes or until the apples are tender. Beat or whisk until smooth.
  *OR*: Put all the ingredients into a pan and cook on the hob until apples are tender. Stir frequently.
  Serve in a bowl to accompany pork, sausages, duck, pheasant etc.


## BRAISED BUTTER-BEANS AND SPARE RIBS

4 oz (100 g) dry butter-beans
1 tbsp (15 ml) cooking oil
4 oz (100 g) onion—sliced
1 lb (450 g) Chinese style spare ribs
½ pint (250 ml) water
1 beef stock cube *or* 1 tsp (5 ml) Bovril
½ tsp (2.5 ml) ground coriander
½ tsp (2.5 ml) cumin seeds
1 tsp (5 ml) honey
a shake of pepper
8 oz (200 g) carrots—scraped and sliced
1½ level tsp (7 ml) cornflour
2 tsp (10 ml) water
½ tsp (2.5 ml) salt

Soak the beans overnight in cold water.

Heat the oil in a pan, add the onion and spare ribs and fry until golden. Stir in the water, stock cube and beans.

Bring to the boil, put on the lid and simmer for 15 minutes. Stir in the spices, honey and carrots.

Place in a warmed oven dish, cover and cook at 160°C (325°F, gas 3) for 1 hour.

Blend the cornflour with a little water and stir into the meat. Bring to the boil, stirring well and cook for about 1 minute to thicken. Stir in a little salt to taste.


## SPICED CHICKEN WINGS

2 lb (900 g) chicken wings
2 tbsp (30 ml) vegetable oil
2 tbsp (30 ml) soy sauce
2 tbsp (30 ml) tomato sauce
1 tbsp (15 ml) honey
1 small clove of garlic
¼ tsp mixed spice

Trim the wings. Mix all other ingredients to a sauce. Crush the garlic and add. Put the chicken in a shallow casserole dish large enough to spread it out. Add all of the sauce.

Cook at 180°C (350°F, gas 4) for about $^3/_4$–1 hour. Turn the wings over several times while cooking. Do not let them become too brown. When cooked the sauce should be caramel red.

Serve hot with vegetables or salad.


## CHICKEN IN A TANGY SAUCE

2 chicken breast fillets
1 tbsp (15 ml) wine vinegar
½ tsp (2.5 ml) Dijon mustard
1 crushed garlic clove
1 tbsp (15 ml) honey
1 tbsp (15 ml) tomato ketchup
1 tbsp (15 ml) soy sauce
a few drops of Worcester sauce
oil for cooking

Blend all the dressing ingredients and cut the chicken pieces in halves lengthways.

Heat the oil in a pan and fry the chicken until tender *or* place the chicken in a dish, brush with oil and cook in a moderate oven until tender.

Drain off the oil and place the chicken on a warmed dish. Heat the dressing and pour evenly over the meat.

Serve with hot vegetables or a salad.

## GRILLED CHICKEN (a quickly made dish)

4 chicken joints
2 level tbsp (15 ml) curry powder
3 tbsp (45 ml) honey
3 tbsp (45 ml) french mustard

Wash the chicken pieces and rub curry powder over them, mix the honey, mustard and remaining curry powder and brush over the meat.

Place in a grill pan and grill for about 20 minutes, or until tender. Turn over several times during the cooking and baste with the juices. Serve hot or cold, with rice or salad.

## PHEASANT WITH CRANBERRY STUFFING

2 pheasants (oven ready)
4 oz (100 g) cranberries (fresh or frozen)
1 chopped onion
2 tbsp (30 ml) port or red wine
2 apples or firm pears
2 oz (50 g) fresh breadcrumbs
salt and pepper
2 bay leaves
3 tbsp honey
4 rashers bacon

Prepare and clean the pheasants. Cook the cranberries and onion in a pan with a little water until the onion is soft. Chop the fruit. Mix the honey, wine, fruit and breadcrumbs with the onions and cranberries. Add a little seasoning. Spoon this stuffing into the body cavity of the birds and put them into a casserole or oven dish. Cut the rind off the bacon and lay it on top of the birds with a bayleaf under them. Roast at 180°C (350°F, gas 4) for about one hour or until the birds are tender. Remove the bacon and cook the birds for another 5 minutes until brown on top. Transfer to a serving dish and keep warm.

*Sauce*
2 tbsp (30 ml) flour
½ pint (250 ml) red wine (could be home made dry red wine)
¼ pint (150 ml) hot water

Chop the bacon add it to the cooking juices from the birds, stir in the flour add the wine and hot water and cook in a pan until it thickens and comes to the boil. Serve as gravy with the sliced meat.

This recipe could also be used with guinea fowl.

## CHICKEN IN SPICY MAYONNAISE (served cold)

3 lb (1½ kg) cooked chicken—cut into bite size pieces

*Sauce*
1 tbsp (15 ml) sunflower oil
1 small chopped onion
1 rounded tbsp (30 ml) tomato puree
1 rounded tbsp (30 ml) apricot jam
1 rounded tbsp (30 ml) honey
½ pint (250 ml) mayonnaise
1 level tbsp (15 ml) curry powder
¼ pint (125 ml) chicken stock
juice of half a lemon
3 tbsp (45 ml) cream or yoghurt

Heat the oil, cook the onion until soft. Stir in the curry powder and cook for a few minutes. Stir in the stock, puree, juice, honey and jam, stir and simmer for 5 minutes.

Remove from the heat and leave to cool. Stir in the mayonnaise and cream or yoghurt. Coat the chicken pieces with the sauce.

Garnish with grapes, salad etc.

# SAUSAGE ROLLS WITH HONEY AND APPLE TOPPING

1 lb (450 g) pork sausage meat
½ lb (225 g) puff pastry
(See recipe for Greek style almond rolls, page 44)
1 tbsp (15 ml) honey
1 tbsp (15 ml) apple juice

Roll out the pastry, roll the sausage meat into rolls 1″ (2.5 cm) in diameter. Dip hands in flour to prevent sticking.

Lay the sausages on the pastry and roll up. Brush the join with water and place onto baking sheet with the join on the underside. Mark into rolls about 1½–2″ (3–5 cm) long. Bake at 200°C (400°F, gas 6) for about 20 minutes until golden brown.

Mix the honey and apple juice together. Warm it in a pan and brush over the sausage rolls while they are hot.

# FISH

# MARINATED MACKEREL, PILCHARD, HERRING etc.

4 cleaned and gutted fish
4 bayleaves
10 black peppercorns
1 dsp (10 ml) honey
5 fl oz (125 ml) white vinegar
5 fl oz (125 ml) milkless cold tea

Lay the fish with a bayleaf on each one in a casserole large enough to lay them flat. Mix vinegar, and tea, add the honey and peppercorns and beat until well mixed. Pour over the fish. Cover with a lid or foil and bake in the oven at 180°C (350°F, gas 4) for 45 to 60 minutes or until well cooked.

Leave to cool in the juices, which will be jellied. Serve cold with bread, rolls, salad, etc.

## VIETNAMESE STYLE STIR-FRIED PRAWNS

2 tbsps vegetable oil
1 lb (450 g) uncooked peeled prawns (the larger, the better)
1 thinly sliced onion
5 garlic cloves
a peeled and grated piece of root ginger (about a tablespoonful)
1 red pepper, deseeded
2 tbsps honey
1 tbsp fish sauce
½ tsp five spice powder
freshly ground black pepper

Heat 1 tablespoon of the oil in a frying pan or wok. Add the prawns and stir until pink in colour (about 1 minute). Remove the prawns with a slotted spoon and add the rest of the oil to the pan.

Stir fry the onion, garlic and ginger for about 3 minutes over high heat, until they are softened and slightly brown. Add the red pepper and cook for a further minute.

Reduce the heat a little and stir in the prawns and the rest of the ingredients. Stir until evenly glazed and cook for a further 2–4 minutes depending on the thickness of the prawns.

## YEAST AND BREAD

Dried yeasts may be used in these recipes but for best results and flavour use fresh yeast—obtainable from supermarkets and bakers who bake on the premises.

## BREAD

1½ lb (750 g) strong plain flour
1 tsp (5 ml) salt
1 oz (25 g) lard or margarine
½ oz (15 g) yeast
1 tsp honey
³/₄ pint (450 ml) water

Blend the yeast with the honey and a little warm water and leave until frothy. Put the flour and salt into a warmed bowl. Warm the water and add a to well in the centre of the flour with the yeast. Mix with the hands, and knead for 5–10 minutes until it has formed a soft elastic dough.

Cover and leave to rise in a warm place until doubled in size (about 45 minutes). Re-knead the dough and cut in 2 equal pieces to fill 2 × 1 lb

(½ kilo) tins. Brush tops with oil (or dust with flour) and leave in a warm place to rise until the dough has doubled in size and is just above the top of the tins (approx 1 hour). Bake at 230°C (450°F, gas 8) for 30–40 minutes until well browned and the loaves sound hollow when tapped. Cool on a rack.


## BAPS

**3 lb (1.5 kg) strong plain flour**
**1½ pints (1 litre) milk and water mixed**
**6 oz (150 g) margarine**
**1½ tsp (30 ml) salt**
**1 oz (25 g) yeast**
**1 level tablespoon (15 ml) honey**

Mix the yeast and honey and leave in a warm place until frothy. Warm the milk and water in a pan to just below boiling point. Remove from the heat, stir in the margarine until melted. Leave to cool until lukewarm. Sieve the flour and salt into a bowl, add the yeast and honey and mix well, stir in the cooled milk mixture. Mix with the hands until a dough is formed then turn out and knead for 10 to 20 minutes until the dough is smooth and elastic. Return to the bowl, cover and leave in a warm place until doubled in size.

Shape into about 24 baps, place on floured baking trays and dust them with flour. Cover and leave in a warm place until doubled in size. Put in a pre-heated oven to 220°C (425°F, gas 7) and bake for 15 mins. Reduce heat to 200°C (400°F, gas 6) and bake for a further 10 minutes.

Cool on a wire rack.

These will keep well in a freezer if packed tightly into plastic bags.


## BARA BRITH

**12 oz (300 g) strong white flour**
**2 oz (50 g) butter or margarine**
**3 tbsp (45 ml) honey (liquid)**
**½ oz (15 g) yeast**
**1 tsp (5 ml) mixed spice**
**2 oz (50 g) currants**
**2 oz (50 g) raisins**
**2 oz (50 g) candied peel**
**4 fl oz (100 ml) milk**
**1 egg**

Blend the yeast with the honey and leave in a warm place until frothy. Rub the margarine into the flour, stir in the yeast and honey, spice and fruit. Warm the milk a little, pour into the dry ingredients with beaten egg. Mix to a stiff dough. Turn onto a board and knead until it feels elastic. Cover with a damp cloth and leave in a warm place until doubled in size.

Grease and line a 2 lb loaf tin. Turn out the dough and knead a little to release the gas. Press the dough into the tin and cover with a damp cloth. Leave in a warm place until well risen.

Bake at 180°C (350°F, gas 4) until it has browned and sounds hollow when tapped. Serve in thin slices spread with butter.

If using dried yeast add it to the warm milk and leave until it is frothy on top. Then add to the flour mixture.


## MILK LOAF

**1 lb (450 g) strong white flour**
**1 tsp (5 ml) salt**
**2 oz (50 g) butter or margarine**
**2 tsp (10 ml) honey**
**1 sachet easy blend yeast or ½ oz (15 g) fresh yeast**
**½ pt (300 ml) milk**
**1 tbsp (15 ml) sesame seeds or poppy seeds (optional)**

Place flour and salt in a bowl and rub in the fat. Warm the milk with the honey until lukewarm. Crumble in the yeast. (If using dried yeast sprinkle it over the milk and leave until frothy. Add the honey, slightly warmed, before adding to the flour.)

Follow the recipe for Bara Brith until the dough has risen for the second time.

Grease and line a loaf tin—or two small ones.

Brush the loaf with a little water and sprinkle on the sesame or poppy seeds. Bake at 230°C (450°F, gas 8) until firm and browned—15 to 20 minutes.

*MILK ROLLS.* Allow the dough to rise once. Divide the dough into small pieces and shape into plaits, twists, crescents etc. Leave on a greased baking tin until doubled in size. Glaze with milk or beaten egg and bake at 225°C (450°F, gas 8) until well risen and golden brown. They should sound hollow when tapped.

# LARDY CAKE

1 lb (450 g) strong flour
1 pkt easy blend yeast or
  ½ oz (15 g) fresh yeast
a pinch of salt
2 tsp (10 ml) sugar
1 egg
8 fl oz (225 ml) milk

*Filling*
4 oz (50 g) lard or cooking fat
4 oz (50 g) currants
4 oz (50 g) honey

Sift the flour and put in a mixing bowl with the salt, easy blend yeast and sugar. Slightly warm the milk and add to the flour with the beaten egg. OR if using fresh yeast, cream it with the sugar add it to the warmed milk and leave until it froths on top before adding to the flour.

Knead until it feels elastic then place in a greased bowl, cover with a damp cloth and leave until it has doubled in size.

Roll out the dough on a floured board to ½" (1 cm) thick.

Mix the filling ingredients and spread half of it onto two thirds of the dough. Fold into three layers and roll out again. Spread on the rest of the filling, refold it and roll out twice more. Shape to fit two 8" (20 cm) cake tins. Leave in a warm place until well risen, then bake in a hot oven 200°C (400°F, gas 6) for about 30 minutes, until browned and firm.

These loaves will keep well if wrapped in plastic and sealed and put in the deep freeze.


# CHELSEA BUNS

8 oz (200 g) strong white flour
½ tsp (2.5 ml) salt
1 tsp (5 ml) honey
1 sachet easy blend yeast or
  ½ oz (15 g) fresh yeast
¼ pt milk (150 ml)

*Filling*
4 oz (100 g) dried fruit
  (currants and sultanas)
1 tsp (5 ml) mixed spice
2 oz (50 g) soft brown sugar
2 tbsp (30 ml) honey

Place flour, salt and sugar in a bowl. (Follow the recipe for Bara Brith until the dough has risen for a second time.)

Place the dough on a board and roll out to an oblong shape—about 10" by 8" (25 × 20 cms).

Mix the fruit with the spice and sugar and spread over the dough, leaving a gap at the edges. Roll up the dough from a narrow end, pinch the edges to stop the fruit coming out. Cut into eight slices. Place these on a greased circular dish or baking tray and leave in a warm place until they have doubled in size and are touching each other.

Bake at 240°C (475°F, gas 9) until well risen and golden brown and firm. Carefully lift the ring of buns onto a rack to cool. While still hot glaze with the warmed honey using a pastry brush. Separate when cool.

## FRUIT AND NUT TEA BREAD

8 oz (200 g) self-raising flour
½ tsp (2.5 ml) mixed spice
4 oz (100 g) margarine
2 oz (50 g) soft brown sugar
2 oz (50 g) chopped nuts
6 oz (150 g) mixed dried fruit (currants, raisins, sultanas)
1 tbsp (15 ml) milk
2 eggs (medium size)
4 tbsp (60 ml) honey

Sieve the flour and spice into a bowl. Rub in the fat, stir in the sugar, nuts, dried fruit, eggs and honey and mix well. Put into a greased and lined loaf tin, 9″ × 5″ (23 cm × 13 cm). Bake for 1–1¼ hours at 180°C (350°F, gas 4), cover top with cooking foil halfway through cooking if it is getting too brown. Cook until firm. Cool slightly on rack and brush with honey. Serve sliced and buttered.

## PUDDINGS AND DESSERTS

## PEARS WITH ORANGE AND CHOCOLATE SAUCE (for 2)

1 orange
1 tbsp (15 ml) water
1 tbsp (15 ml) honey
2 firm but ripe pears
1 oz (25 g) plain chocolate—grated

Scrape the rind from the orange and extract the juice. Into a small saucepan put the water, orange juice, rind and honey.

Cut the pears in halves lengthwise and remove the core and skin. Warm the orange juice and honey, add the pears, cover and simmer on very low heat for 10–15 minutes, until just soft but not 'mushy'.

Remove the pears from the syrup and place on a cooling rack or colander over a plate.

Boil the syrup rapidly for about 1 minute, until reduced.

Remove from the heat and add the chocolate.

Stir well and leave to cool.

To serve: Put 2 pear halves in each serving dish and pour the chocolate sauce over them.

## PEACHES WITH ALMONDS (for 2)

**2 medium sized peaches**
**a few fresh raspberries or strawberries or 4 tsp (20 ml) jam**
**4 oz (100 g) Greek style yoghurt**
**2 tsp honey**
**2–3 drops of almond essence**
**1 oz (25 g) flaked almonds**

Halve the peaches and remove the stones. Brush with lemon juice to prevent discoloration. Spoon jam or fresh fruit into the stone cavity.

Mix together the yoghurt, honey and essence. Toast the nuts until golden and chop about $^3/_4$ of them.

Stir the nuts into the yoghurt.

Spoon the mixture onto the peach halves and decorate with almond flakes.

## BANANA LONGBOAT (for 4)

**2 tbsp (60 ml) honey**
**4 bananas**
**1 small tin of fruit cocktail**
**1 small carton whipping cream**
**Chocolate vermicelli or chopped roasted almonds**
**4 oval dishes to serve**

Put a tbsp of fruit cocktail into each dish.

Cut the bananas in halves lengthwise after removing the skins.

Place on top of the fruit.

Whip the cream and pipe it on to the bananas.

Decorate with chocolate vermicelli or grated chocolate. Dribble a tsp of honey on to each banana slice. Keep cool until served.

# BANANAS IN SULTANA AND RUM SAUCE

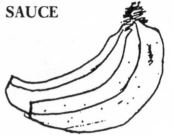

2 oz (50 g) sultanas
2 fl oz (50 ml) rum
3 tbsp (45 ml) honey
3 tbsp (45 ml) lemon juice
1½ oz (37 g) butter or margarine
4 bananas

Put all the ingredients except the bananas in a pan and heat until blended and the butter melted.

Cut the bananas into slices and lay in a shallow dish.

Pour the sauce over the top of the fruit.

Cover with foil and bake in moderate oven 180°C (350°F, gas 4) for about 12–15 minutes until the bananas are slightly soft.

Serve with cream or yoghurt.


# GRAPES IN HONEY SAUCE

1 tbsp (15 ml) honey
2 tbsp (30 ml) brandy
1 tsp (5 ml) lemon juice
a bunch of seedless grapes

Place the honey, lemon and brandy in a pan and warm gently until blended.

Wash the grapes and place in a bowl. Pour the sauce over them. See they are all covered then put in a refrigerator to cool.

Serve in small dishes with cream, yoghurt or custard.


# DRIED FRUIT SALAD

8 oz (200 g) mixed dried fruits (apple, apricots, prunes, pears, etc)
4 fl oz (100 ml) cold tea
4 fl oz (100 ml) water
2 tbsp (30 ml) honey
2 tsp (10 ml) lemon juice
a small cinnamon stick
4 cloves

Mix the fruit with the water, tea, honey, lemon and spices.

Cover and leave to soak for at least 2 hours (it could be left overnight).

Cook in a pan until the fruit is tender, stirring occasionally.

Remove the cinnamon and cloves. Leave to stand.
Serve warm with custard, or cold with cream, yoghurt or ice cream.

## GOOSEBERRY PUREE

1 lb (450 g) gooseberries
2 tbsp (30 ml) honey
6 tbsp (90 ml) dry white wine, home made elderflower or
   gooseberry or water
1 sprig of elderflower (if in season) or dried elderflowers

Put the gooseberries and wine (or water) in a saucepan and cook slowly with
the lid on until quite soft. Cool slightly.
   Rub the mixture through a sieve or strainer.
   Add the honey, stirring until well mixed.
   Use for a sundae with cream, yoghurt and sponge fingers, or as a filling for
a sponge flan.

## FIGS WITH HONEY

Fresh figs, or dried figs (soaked in water until soft)
Grated rind and juice of orange (1 orange will do 8 figs)
Grated cardamom
1 level tsp honey to each fig

Cut the figs in half and lay skin side down in a baking dish.
   Sprinkle with cardamom.
   Cook in a warm oven or microwave until tender.
   Make honey syrup using orange juice, grated orange rind and honey
blended in a bowl or jug and warmed.
   Pour over the figs while they are still hot.
   Serve hot or cold with plain yoghurt, custard, cream or ice cream.
   Or:
   Put figs in a circle on a sponge flan. Thicken the syrup by adding cornflour
and warming until clear. Pour the syrup evenly over the figs.

## LEMON SNOW

Rind and juice of 1½ lemons
1½ tbsp honey
½ pint (250 ml) water
½ oz (12 g) gelatine
1 egg white

Thinly peel the lemon. Put rind in a small pan with the water. Bring to the boil and strain onto the gelatine. Stir until dissolved.

Stir in the honey and allow to cool. Chill until just beginning to set.

Whisk the egg white until stiff, add lemon juice and whisk again.

Pour into a dish and leave to set in a refrigerator

## CHOCOLATE FUDGE SUNDAE (for 2)

1½ oz (37 g) plain chocolate
³/₄ oz (20 g) butter or margarine
2 fl oz (50 ml) milk
6 oz (150 g) soft brown sugar
1 tbsp (15 ml) honey
2 large ripe bananas
2 peaches
2 scoops of vanilla ice cream
a few chopped nuts
glace cherries to decorate

Melt the chocolate and fat in a pan on the hotplate, cook until hot and bubbly, stirring to prevent burning.

Add the sugar stirring well and cook until bubbling.

Remove from the heat and stir in the honey.

Put the bananas—sliced, and the peaches, peeled and sliced, in sundae glasses. Put the ice cream on top.

Pour the fudge sauce over the ice cream, sprinkle with nuts and decorate with a cherry.

Serve at once.

## PEARS WITH CHOCOLATE SAUCE

2 large or 4 small dessert pears
8 fl oz (200 ml) water
2 oz (50 g) honey
1 vanilla pod
2 cloves

*Sauce*
4 oz (100 g) plain chocolate
2 tbsp (30 ml) water
½ oz (12 g) butter or margarine
1 tbsp (15 ml) yoghurt or cream

Peel the pears, leaving the stalks on. Cut a slice off the bottoms so that they stand upright.

Put the honey, water, vanilla and cloves in a pan and simmer for 1 minute. Stand the pears in this and poach for 15–20 minutes until tender (keeping them upright). Lift out the pears and stand in a serving dish. Just melt the chocolate in the water, add the butter and cream and beat until smooth.

Pour the sauce over the pears and serve quickly.

## PLUM SAUCE WITH ORANGE

**8 oz (225 g) ripe plums**
**2 tbsp (30 ml) honey**
**a few strips of orange rind**
**4 tbsp (60 ml) orange juice**

Put the plums, orange peel and juice into a pan and simmer until soft (about 5 minutes). Remove the stones and the orange rind. Add the honey.

Blend by hand or in a mixer to a soft puree, adding more honey if not sweet enough.

Serve warm with sponge pudding or milk puddings.

Serve cold with ice cream, yoghurt or cornflour blancmange.

Greengages or damsons could also be used.

## CROWDIE (serves 4)

**2 oz (50 g) medium oatmeal**
**10 fl oz (300 ml) double cream**
**4 tbsp (60 ml) liquid honey**
**3 tbsp (45 ml) whisky**
**12 oz (350 g) fresh raspberries**

Spread the oatmeal in a grill pan and toast until golden brown, turning occasionally. Leave to cool.

Whip the cream until stiff, then stir in the honey, whisky and oatmeal. Put layers of the cream mixture and raspberries into four tall glasses, cover with cling film and put into a refrigerator. Allow to come to room temperature (about 30 minutes) before serving.

Decorate with a few raspberries.

## APPLE JELLY

2 lb (900 g) cooking apples
2 oz (50 g) sugar
2 oz (50 g) honey
½ pint (250 ml) water
1 orange or lime jelly

Dissolve the sugar in the water. Add the chopped, peeled and cored apples and cook until tender.

Break the jelly into pieces and stir into the apple mixture until dissolved. Stir in the honey and mix well. Pour into a dish and cool or chill until set.

Serve with cream or ice cream. (The jelly is best made several hours before serving, or made the previous day in warm weather.)

## APPLE CRUNCH

1½ lb (650 g) cooking apples
2 tbsp (30 ml) honey
1 tsp (5 ml) cinnamon
2 tbsp (30 ml) water

*Topping*
3 oz (75 g) porridge oats
2 oz (50 g) soft brown sugar
1 oz (25 g) wholemeal flour
1½ oz (37 g) melted margarine

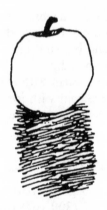

Grease a pie dish. Peel and slice the apples. Warm the water and mix with the honey and cinnamon.

Put the apples in the dish with the honey mixture spread evenly over them. Mix the oats, sugar and flour, stir in the melted margarine and mix well. Sprinkle this evenly over the apples.

Bake for 50–60 minutes at 180°C (350°F, gas 4) until the apples are soft and topping is crisp. Serve warm.

## HONEY AND APPLE TART

12 oz (300 g) cooking apples
4 oz (100 g) honey
Juice and rind of 1 lemon
9 oz (225 g) shortcrust pastry
(6 oz (150 g) flour, 3 oz (75 g) fat and water to mix)

Peel and core the apples. Put in a pan with the lemon juice. Cook slowly, stirring occasionally until the apples are soft. (A little water may be needed if the apples are dry.) Remove from hob.

Stir in the honey then add the breadcrumbs. Stir until mixed.

Roll out the pastry and line a 8" (20 cm) flan tin. Spoon the apple mixture into the centre and level the surface.

Cook in the oven at 190°C (375°F, gas 5) for 30–35 minutes until it is firm to the touch. Serve warm or cold.


# APPLE AND HONEY CHEESECAKE

*Crumb base and topping*
6 oz (175 g) digestive biscuits
3 oz (75 g) butter

*Filling*
$^3/_4$ pint (400 ml) apple puree (made from 1½ lb (675 g) apples)
2 tbsp (30 ml) honey
½ oz (15 g) packet of powdered gelatine
½ pint (250 ml) carton fresh double cream (or fromage frais)

Lightly butter a 7½" (19 cm) tin and line with greaseproof paper. Crush the biscuits and mix with the melted butter. Set aside 3 tablespoons of the mixture and press the rest into the prepared tin. Heat the apple puree with the honey until it has dissolved.

Dissolve the gelatine in a little cold water, stir into the apple puree and leave to cool. Whip the cream, if using, until stiff enough to hold its shape and fold the cream or fromage frais into the apple mixture.

Pour onto the biscuit base, scatter remaining biscuit mix on top and leave to set.


# GOOSEBERRY FOOL

½ lb (200 g) gooseberries—topped and tailed
2 tsp (10 ml) water
2 tsp (20 ml) honey
2 tsp (20 ml) sugar
3 tbsp (45 ml) double cream or Greek yoghurt
¼ pint (125 ml) custard
chopped nuts to decorate

Put the fruit, sugar, honey and water in a pan or bowl and cook until tender. When cool, puree in a blender or strain through a sieve using a wooden spoon to press it. Whip the cream until stiff, then fold in the fruit and the custard *or* fold the fruit into the yoghurt and custard.

Put into serving bowl and sprinkle nuts on top.


## FROZEN APRICOT SWEET

1 can of apricots (unsweetened if possible)
 or $^3/_4$ lb (300 g) fresh apricots with stone removed and
  lightly poached
 or dried apricots, soaked for at least 8 hours and lightly
  cooked with a dessertspoon (10 ml) sugar
4 fl oz (125 ml) yoghurt
1 tbsp (15 ml) honey (reduce honey if sweetened apricots are
 used)

Drain the apricots. Process in a mixer until coarsely chopped (or chop by hand). Stir in the honey and yoghurt and mix well. Place in a freezer container, cover, and freeze until firm.

Break into pieces, and process in a mixer until smooth and foamy. Pour back into the container, cover and freeze until firm. Serve cold.

Peaches could be used instead of apricots.


## BLACKCURRANT AND PEACH DESSERT

8 oz (200 g) blackcurrants
2 tbsp (30 ml) honey
2 tsp (10 ml) lemon juice
8 tbsp (120 ml) water
½ oz (12 g) cornflour
2 fresh peaches (or tinned)

Cook the blackcurrants with the lemon juice in the water until tender.

Puree in a blender and sieve to remove pips and skin.

Mix the cornflour to a paste with some of the juice and cook until thickened, stirring well. Stir in the honey and mix well.

Spoon into a serving dish and arrange thinly cut peach slices on top.

Keep cool and serve with yoghurt or ice cream.

## STRAWBERRIES WITH PORT (serves 4)

1 lb (450 g) strawberries
2 fl oz (50 ml) port wine (or red wine)
2 tbsp (30 ml) honey (clear and light)

Remove the stalks from the strawberries. Put a quarter of them in a bowl and mash until pulpy.
    Add the wine and honey and mix well with a fork.
    Put in refrigerator to chill.
    Divide the rest of the strawberries into four bowls and spoon the sauce over the top.
    Serve with cream, ice cream or yoghurt.
    Could also be made with raspberries.


## RASPBERRY SYLLABUB (for 4)

½ pint (275 ml) thick cream
2 tbsp (30 ml) brandy or whisky
1 tbsp (15 ml) honey
8 oz (200 g) raspberries

Whip the cream until stiff, whip in the spirit and honey.
    Fold in the raspberries and divide the mixture between four chilled glasses.
    Keep cool until serving.
    This could also be made with small strawberries.


## BANANA SYLLABUB

3 large or 4 smaller bananas
2 tbsp (30 ml) honey
2 tbsp (30 ml) lemon juice
1 tbsp (15 ml) brandy
½ pint (250 ml) cream
chocolate (flaked) or chopped nuts to decorate

Mash the bananas, honey and lemon juice together. Whip the cream until it is stiff. Stir in the banana mixture and blend well. Add the brandy and stir in. Pour into a bowl or six sundae dishes.
    Smooth the top and decorate with grated chocolate or nuts.
    Keep cool and serve cold.

## SCOTTISH CREAM

1 pint (600 ml) milk
a good pinch of mixed spice
2 oz (60 g) porridge oats
3 tbsp (45 ml) honey
3 tbsp (45 ml) whisky
4 oz (100 g) yoghurt or fromage frais

Heat the milk and mixed spice. Stir in the porridge oats and simmer until thick (about 10 minutes). Stir to prevent burning. Remove from the heat and leave to cool.

Stir in all the honey except 1 teaspoon, add the whisky, mix well and leave to cool. Stir in the yoghurt or fromage frais. Put in the refrigerator to cool.

Serve cold with a drizzle of honey on the top.


## HONEY APRICOT WHIPS

4 oz (100 g) dried apricots
½ pint (250 ml) hot water
2 tbsp (30 ml) honey
10 oz (250 g) yoghurt
2 egg whites (or equivalent in sterilised or powdered egg white)
boudoir biscuits, or sponge fingers to serve

Wash the apricots. Pour the hot water over them and leave for 5–6 hours or overnight. Turn into a pan and simmer for about 20 minutes or until soft. Add the honey and stir in well. Remove from the heat and leave until cold.

Add the yoghurt and puree in a blender or with a hand-whisk. Whisk the egg whites until stiff and fold into the mixture.

Spoon into sundae glasses and serve at once, with biscuits or refrigerate until required.


## BANANA CREAM

¼ oz (6 g) gelatine
¼ pint (125 ml) milk (fresh or tinned evaporated)
6 bananas
2 oz (50 g) honey
½ pint (250 ml) double cream or ½ pint (250 ml) Greek style
  yoghurt

Dissolve the gelatine in warm milk and leave to cool (not to set).

Slice or mash the bananas with the honey. Whip the cream until thick and fold into the banana mixture *or* fold the yoghurt into the bananas without whipping. Leave in a refrigerator until set and serve with biscuits.

## HONEY LEMON CREAM PIE

2 oz (50 g) margarine
4 oz (100 g) digestive biscuits
1 oz (25 g) soft brown sugar
1 small can evaporated milk (chilled)
finely grated rind and juice of 1 large lemon
1 tbsp (15 ml) honey
2 tbsp (30 ml) water
½ oz (12 g) gelatine
a small piece of chocolate

Melt the fat in the pan, remove from the heat and stir in the finely crushed biscuits and the sugar. Tip it into a loose bottomed 7″ (18 cm) flan tin and put into a refrigerator for ½ hour.

Whisk the milk until thick, add the lemon rind, the juice and the honey and whisk again.

Put the water into a small bowl and sprinkle the gelatine on it. When it is well mixed, stand the bowl in hot water and stir until it is dissolved.

Strain into the lemon mixture, whisk well and pour on to the biscuit mixture. Put into the refrigerator until it is set. Serve cold, decorated with grated chocolate.

This flan is suitable for freezing. Open freeze in the freezer, remove from the tin and wrap in foil and plastic. Seal and return to the freezer. On removal, let it thaw for 1½–2 hours. Do not add the chocolate until after thawing.

## APPLE FLAPJACK PUDDING

6 oz (150 g) peeled and sliced apples
3 oz (75 g) blackberries
2 tbsp (30 ml) honey
1 tbsp (15 ml) margarine
2 oz (50 g) porridge oats

Put the fruit in a souffle dish or pie dish. Dribble 1 tablespoon (15 ml) honey evenly over the top. Warm the rest of the honey and margarine in a pan over low heat until melted. Add the oats and mix well.

Sprinkle the honeyed oats over the fruit and lightly smooth the top. Bake at 180°C (350°F, gas 4) for about 25 minutes.

Serve hot or cold.

## APPLE MERINGUE PIE

*Pastry*
6 oz (150 g) plain flour
3 oz (75 g) margarine or cooking fat
water to mix

Rub fat into flour, add enough water to bind. Roll out and line a 7" (18 cm) flan dish. Bake at 200°C (400°F, gas 6) until lightly cooked.

*Filling*
2 large cooking apples
1 large egg—separated
2 oz (50 g) caster sugar
2 tbsp (30 ml) honey

Peel, core and slice the apples. Cook in a pan in very little water until soft. Allow to cool slightly. Beat the egg yolk into the apple with the honey. Test for sweetness and add more honey if needed. Whisk the egg white until stiff then fold in with the caster sugar. Spread the apple puree into the flan, then spread the meringue mixture on top.

Bake at 180°C (350°F, gas 4) for about 20 minutes until the meringue is lightly browned.

## OPEN CHERRY PIE

*Pastry*
6 oz (150 g) plain flour
3 oz (75 g) margarine or cooking fat
water to mix

Rub fat into flour, add enough water to bind. Roll out and line a 7" (18 cm) flan dish. Bake at 200°C (400°F, gas 6) until cooked.

*Filling*
1 tin of black cherries
1 oz (25 g) cornflour or arrowroot
2 tbsp (30 ml) honey

Strain the cherries. Put the cornflour into a pan and mix with a small amount of cherry juice until dissolved. Add the rest of the juice and the honey. Stir well. Heat until it comes to the boil (it should become clear). Put aside to cool. Pour the cherry mixture into the flan and smooth the top. Leave in a cool place to set.

Serve plain or with cream or yoghurt.

## GOOSEBERRY RING (serves 4)

1 pint (500 ml) milk
2 oz (50 g) semolina
1 tbsp (15 ml) honey
2 eggs—separated
1 lb (450 g) gooseberries
grated lemon rind (optional)

Warm the milk, sprinkle in the semolina and mix well. Simmer until thick, add the honey and lemon rind. Remove from the heat and stir in the egg yolks mixing well.

Cook the gooseberries until soft. If they seem sharp to taste add a little honey and puree them until well mixed. Whisk the egg whites until stiff and fold into the semolina with the gooseberries. Pour into a wetted mould and leave to set. Chill before serving.

If the gooseberries are ripe and sweet, reserve a few for decorating the pudding.

## BANANA AND APRICOT BREAD AND BUTTER PUDDING (serves 4)

5 slices of white bread
1 oz (25 g) butter or margarine
2 oz (50 g) dried apricots (soaked overnight)
2 bananas (sliced)
1 oz (25 g) raisins
1 tbsp (15 ml) honey
½ tsp (2.5 ml) cinnamon (optional)
2 eggs (medium size)
³/₄ pint (400 ml) milk

Spread the fat on to the bread, cut off any hard crusts and cut bread into small pieces. Chop the apricots and mix with the sliced bananas and raisins. Mix the cinnamon with the honey and add to the fruit.

Place the bread and fruit in layers in a deep pie dish with a layer of bread (buttered side up) on the top. Beat the eggs with the milk and pour over the mixture in the dish.

Cook at 180°C (350°F, gas 4) for 35–40 minutes until golden on top.


## MIXED FRUIT BRULEE (serves 4–6)

1 banana
1 peach (large or 2 small)
a small bunch of grapes
2 tangerine oranges or clementines
a slice of ripe melon
a few strawberries or raspberries
4 tbsp (60 ml) yoghurt
a few flaked almonds
2 oz (50 g) sugar
3 fl oz (75 ml) water
1 tbsp (15 ml) honey

Divide the fruit into individual serving dishes. Pour a teaspoon (5 ml) honey over each. Spread a tablespoon (15 ml) yoghurt mixed with the almonds over each dish.

Dissolve the sugar in the water, bring to the boil and cook rapidly for about five minutes until it forms a brown caramel. Pour a thin layer over each dish and leave to cool before serving.

The fruit can be varied according to season.


## GREEK STYLE ALMOND ROLLS

*A quickly made sweet for a dinner party*
½ lb (200 g) packet of puff pastry
1 lb (400 g) almond paste or marzipan
2 tbsp (30 ml) honey
2 tbsp (30 ml) orange juice

Roll out the pastry into a rectangle. Knead the almond paste until soft then roll it with the hands into a long sausage shape. Place the almond paste on the pastry, roll the pastry over, wet and seal the edges. Cut into 2" (5 cm) lengths and place on a baking tray, with the pastry join underneath. Bake at 220°C (425°F, gas 7) for about 15 minutes.

Warm the honey and orange juice until blended. Serve the rolls hot and hand the sauce round separately.

Although this is a quick recipe using ready-made ingredients, the puff pastry and almond paste may be made at home as follows.

*Puff Pastry*
4 oz (100 g) flour
3 oz (75 g) margarine or cooking fat
a little lemon juice
cold water to mix

Sift the flour into a bowl, soften the fat and add a quarter of it to the flour. Mix to a stiff consistency with the lemon juice and water.

Knead on a lightly floured board then roll into an oblong shape.

Flake another quarter of the fat on to it, covering two-thirds of the length and leaving the edges clear half an inch. Fold the pastry into three layers, sealing the edges with the rolling pin. Repeat this twice more, turning the pastry a quarter turn each time. Leave in a cool place for at least half an hour before using.

*Almond Paste*
½ lb (200 g) icing sugar
½ lb (200 g) ground almonds
1 egg—lightly beaten
½ tsp (2.5 ml) vanilla essence
lemon juice

Sift the sugar into a bowl, add the almonds, egg and essence. Add enough lemon juice to make a stiff dough. Knead well.


## RASPBERRY CHEESECAKE

*Base*
2 oz (50 g) butter or margarine
1 dsp (10 ml) honey
6 oz (150 g) porridge oats

*Filling*
8 oz (200 g) cream cheese
3 tbsp (45 ml) honey
4 fl oz (100 ml) raspberry yoghurt
4 fl oz (100 ml) soured cream or cheese (fromage frais)

*To decorate*
4 oz (100 g) fresh or frozen raspberries

Grease and line an 8" (20 cm) loose bottomed cake tin. Gently heat the margarine and honey in a pan until melted. Remove from the heat and add the oats. Mix well. Spread the mixture evenly into the base of the tin and press it down well with the back of a spoon.

*Topping*: Put the cheese in a mixing bowl, add the honey, yolks of the eggs and yoghurt. Beat until smooth. Whisk the egg whites until stiff and fold into the mixture. Carefully pour on to the base in the tin.

Bake for 45 minutes to 1 hour at 170°C (325°F, gas 3) until just firm.

Spread the soured cream or fromage frais over the top and return to the oven for 5 minutes. Leave the cheesecake in a warm place or in the oven with the door open for about 20 minutes. Remove to a cooler place. Remove from the tin and put on a serving dish. Arrange raspberries on the top.


## HONEY TART

*Pastry base*
6 oz (150 g) plain flour
3 oz (75 g) cooking fat or margarine
water to bind

Rub fat into the sieved flour until it looks like breadcrumbs. Add water until it will bind together. Knead lightly and roll out on to a board. Line a 7–8" (15–16 cm) sponge tin with the pastry. Save surplus pastry for strips.

*Filling*
3 rounded tbsp (80 ml) honey
2 oz (50 g) white breadcrumbs
grated lemon rind
1 tbsp (15 ml) lemon juice

Warm the honey—do not let it get hot. Add the lemon rind and juice and pour on to the breadcrumbs and mix well. Spoon the honey mixture into the pastry, spread evenly. Put pastry strips on top. Cook for 20–25 minutes at 200°C (400°F, gas 6) until the pastry is cooked. Serve warm.


## HAZELNUT TART (serves 6–8)

12 oz (300 g) shortcrust pastry (8 oz (200 g) flour, 4 oz (100 g) fat)
8 oz (200 g) hazelnuts
2 oz (50 g) light brown sugar
2 oz (50 g) butter or margarine
2 large eggs
6 oz (175 g) honey

juice of half a lemon
2 egg whites

Line a 10″ (25 cm) round flan dish with the pastry. Shell and finely chop the hazelnuts. Beat the fat and sugar together and gradually add the beaten eggs. Add honey and lemon juice and beat or whisk until it becomes frothy. Whisk the two egg whites and add the chopped hazelnuts. Pour into the pastry case.

Bake for 10 minutes at 230°C (450°F, gas 8). Reduce heat to 180°C (350°F, gas 4) and bake for about 25 minutes or until the filling is brown on top and set. Serve cold.


## ORANGE AND HONEY SAUCE FOR ICE CREAM

1 rounded tsp (10 ml) cornflour
4 tbsp (60 ml) water
2 oranges or 3 tbsp (45 ml) orange juice
1 tbsp (15 ml) honey
1 tbsp (15 ml) seedless raisins

Mix a teaspoon of water with the cornflour. Stir until smooth. Add the rest of the water. Add the juice of the oranges and heat until it is clear, stirring all the time.

Remove from the heat, stir in the honey and raisins and leave to cool. Refrigerate until required. Serve with ice cream.


## FIG AND ORANGE SWEET

4 fl oz (125 ml) orange juice
2 tbsp (30 ml) lemon juice
2 fl oz (60 ml) honey
4 ripe figs—trimmed and sliced
2 oranges
ground cinnamon

Mix fruit juices and honey well together. Add the sliced figs to the juices and chill. Peel the oranges, remove the pith, pips and the skin surrounding the segments. Chill in fridge.

To serve: Put figs in the bottom of sundae glasses, arrange orange segments around the sides, spoon syrup over and sprinkle with cinnamon.

## WHISKY AND OATMEAL SYLLABUB Serves 4–6

1 tbsp (15 ml) honey
3 tbsp (45 ml) whisky
1 tsp (5 ml) lemon juice
10 fl oz (300 ml) whipping cream
1 oz (25 g) medium oatmeal (toasted)

Mix together the honey, whisky and lemon juice. Fold in the cream and most of the oatmeal.

Pile into grapefruit glasses or sundae dishes, chill and sprinkle the remaining oatmeal on top.

Porridge oats could be used. A few seconds in the liquidiser would reduce the size of the flakes.

## PRESERVES

## GREEK APRICOT MARMALADE

1 lb (400 g) dried apricots
8 oz (200 g) honey
1½ oz (35 g) pistachio nuts—chopped
¼ tsp dried mint
1 tbsp (15 ml) pine nuts

Soak apricots to cover for a few hours or overnight. Drain and cut into small pieces.

In a pan, combine the honey and 4 fl oz (100 ml) of water and bring to the boil. Add chopped apricots and mint and cook until it is a thick syrup. Add nuts and cook for 3–4 minutes.

(Will not keep indefinitely, only a week or two.)

## THERESA'S HONEY MARMALADE

2 lb (1 kg) seville oranges
2 pints (1 litre) water
1½ lb (600 g) honey
2½ lb (1.2 kg) sugar
knob of butter

Wash the fruit, cut oranges in half and extract the flesh. Peel and finely chop the skins. Place in a pressure cooker with 1 pint (500 ml) water and pips tied in muslin. Cook for 20 minutes at 10 lb pressure.

Open the pan, add 1 pint (500 ml) water, the sugar and honey. Stir until sugars have dissolved, then boil rapidly until setting point is reached.

Remove from the heat, stir in the knob of butter to disperse foam.

Leave to stand for 5 minutes then stir to mix in peel before bottling.


## VICTORIAN HONEY CHUTNEY

I am grateful to Jane Jones of International Bee Research Association for this recipe of which she says: "This recipe is an excellent way of using up any honey which may not be up to the most exacting of table standards".

8 oz (225 g) plums (preferably Victoria)
1 lb (450 g) cooking apples (weighed after being peeled and cored)
4 oz (110 g) red tomatoes
8 oz (225 g) raisins
4 large tablespoons of honey
2 oz (50 g) garlic, finely chopped **with 2 oz (50g) onions**
½ tbsp salt
¼ tsp ground ginger
1 oz (25 g) whole mixed spice
½ pint (570 ml) malt vinegar

Chop the plums and tomatoes into medium sized pieces and put into a preserving pan.

Place the onions and apples in a food processor and finely chop.

Add to the pan together with all the other ingredients, make sure the whole spices are securely tied in a muslin bag and suspend from the handle of the pan. Cook the chutney slowly on a low heat for about 45 minutes or until most of the liquid has evaporated. Stir regularly especially towards the end of the cooking time to prevent the mixture sticking to the base of the pan.

Put the chutney while still warm into hot jars and seal immediately.

# SOUP, SALADS AND VEGETABLES

## CARROT SOUP

1 lb (400 g) carrots
2 med. onions sliced
1 bayleaf
1½ pints (750 ml) chicken stock
1 tsp (5 ml) honey
1 large cooking apple
3 oz (75 g) butter or cooking fat
salt and pepper
a squeeze of lemon juice
chopped parsley or chervil

Slice carrots and cook with bayleaf in stock until tender.
   Slice apples and onions and fry in fat. Add to carrots and cook until soft.
Remove bayleaf and liquidise. Add seasoning, honey, lemon juice and parsley.
   OR Cook carrots, onion and apple in microwave until soft and add to
stock.

## CUCUMBER SALAD

1 large cucumber
1 tsp (5 ml) salt
2 tbsp (30 ml) wine vinegar
1 dsp (10 ml) honey
1 medium sized onion
1 clove of garlic—crushed
seasoning
paprika

Thinly slice the cucumber. Sprinkle with salt and leave in a colander to drain
for 1 hour. Dry on a cloth and add to the vinegar, honey, garlic and
seasoning. Thinly slice the onion and separate the rings. Add to the
cucumber and sprinkle with paprika.

## CELERY AND APPLE SALAD

1 head of celery
2 dessert apples

*Honey and lemon dressing*
juice of 1 lemon
2 tbsp (30 ml) honey
salt and pepper to taste

Slice the celery and apples, combine all the dressing ingredients and toss well so that the apples will not brown.


## APPLE, CELERY AND WALNUT SALAD

3 eating apples
juice of 1 lemon (strained)
3 stalks of celery
2 pineapple rings (tinned or fresh)
6 walnut halves—chopped small
4 fl oz (120 ml) mayonnaise
1 tbsp (15 ml) honey

Peel and core the apples and cut celery into pieces. Put into a bowl with the lemon juice and toss until well coated.

Add the chopped celery and walnuts, cut the pineapple rings into small pieces and add. Mix the honey and mayonnaise and fold into the fruit mixture. Cover and chill for several hours.

Remove from fridge and serve at room temperature.


## BEETROOT SALAD

8 oz (225 g) cooked beetroot
1 medium orange
1 medium pear
4 sticks of celery—sliced
2½ fl oz (75 ml) low fat or Greek style yoghurt
1 dsp (10 ml) honey
1 dsp (10 ml) lemon juice
4 tsp (20 ml) chopped chives
lettuce, chicory leaves, watercress etc.

Strain and dice the beetroot. Peel and dice the pear. Remove peel and pith from orange and slice thinly. Mix beetroot, pear, orange, and celery together in a bowl. Mix honey, lemon juice, chives and yoghurt together and mix into the fruit and vegetables.

Arrange leaves round the edge of the dish and spoon the salad into the middle.

# VEGETABLE SALAD WITH HONEY DRESSING

4 oz (100 g) cauliflower florets—cut small pieces
1 courgette—very thinly sliced
3 oz (75 g) peas—lightly cooked
4 oz (100 g) small button mushrooms—sliced
4 oz (100 g) carrots—thinly sliced or grated
2 sticks of celery—cut into thin slices
3 oz (75 g) sweetcorn—lightly cooked or tinned

*Dressing*
2 tbsp (30 ml) honey
1 tbsp (15 ml) white wine vinegar
½ tsp (2.5 ml) strong mustard powder
1 tbsp (15 ml) chopped fresh parsley
salt and pepper

Mix all the vegetables in a bowl. Mix all the dressing ingredients and add to the vegetables. Toss well, chill and serve with cold meat, cheese or smoked fish.


# GINGER AND CHIVE DRESSING

1 tsp (2.5 ml) finely chopped fresh or dry powdered ginger
3 tbsp (45 ml) lemon juice
2 tsp (10 ml) honey
1 tbsp (15 ml) soy sauce
3–4 tbsp (45–60 ml) chopped chives

Mix all together and pour over salad.


# HOT RED CABBAGE AND APPLE SALAD

1 large cooking apple
10 oz (250 g) red cabbage
1 tbsp (15 ml) apple juice
pinch of ground cloves
1 tsp (5 ml) honey
1 tsp (5 ml) cider vinegar
1 tsp (5 ml) apple, redcurrant or quince jelly
½ oz (12 g) margarine or butter

Put shredded cabbage, chopped apple, cider and apple juice in a pan and cook for 15 minutes or put in a covered bowl and microwave on HIGH for 6–8 minutes (stir halfway).

Add cloves, cider vinegar, honey, jelly and fat. Heat in pan until hot, stirring until well blended or microwave for 1½ minutes on HIGH.

Serve hot.


## SPICED RED CABBAGE

1 lb (400 g) red cabbage
1 oz (25 g) butter or margarine
a small onion—chopped
8 oz (200 g) cooking apples—chopped
salt and freshly ground black pepper
nutmeg
2 tbsp (30 ml) water
2 tbsp (30 ml) wine vinegar
1 dsp (10 ml) honey

Cut the cabbage into quarters and discard outer leaves. Shred finely.

Melt fat and fry onion (it could be microwaved until soft). Add apples and cook for 1–2 minutes.

In a casserole put a layer of cabbage then a layer of apple and onion mix. Season well. Add alternate layers until all is in. Mix water, vinegar and honey until smooth. Add to dish.

Cook at 150°C (300°F, gas 2) for about 2 hours. Serve hot or cold.


## GLAZED CARROTS

1lb (400 g) new young carrots
1 dsp (10 ml) honey
1 tbsp (15 ml) butter or margarine
1 tbsp (15 ml) fresh coriander—chopped or minced
half a cup of water

Put honey and water in pan, mix together and add carrots. Cook until the carrots are tender. Save a quarter to an eighth of a cup of liquid. Add the margarine or butter.

When ready to serve, heat up and stir when butter is melting. Roll carrots in it, lift out and serve with fresh coriander.

## VEGETABLE KEBABS

1 large onion cut into wedges
1 red and 1 yellow pepper, deseeded, cored and cut into squares
1 small aubergine cubed
½ lb (225 g) courgettes cut diagonally into 1 in (2.5 cm) pieces
4 oz (125 g) dried apricots

*For the marinade*
3 tbsps each of clear honey, olive oil and red wine vinegar

Thread the prepared vegetables and apricots alternately on to skewers.
Mix together marinade ingredients and place kebabs and marinade into a
shallow dish. Leave to marinade several hours, turning the kebabs occasionally.
   Line a grill pan with foil and place kebabs on to foil. Grind over some fresh
black pepper and grill or barbecue for 6–8 min, turning frequently.
   Brush several times with marinade while cooking.

# DRINKS

## STRAWBERRY COCKTAIL

5 ice cubes
juice of 1 lemon
3 fl oz (75 ml) rum (or dry mead)
2 tsp (10 ml) caster sugar or honey
4 oz (100 g) strawberries

Blend until thick and well combined.

## APRICOT NECTAR

½ pint (300 ml) orange juice
8 apricot halves
1 tbsp (15 ml) lemon juice
1 tbsp (15 ml) honey

Put all the ingredients in a blender and blend for 10–15 seconds.
   Chill well before serving.
   Can be made with 8 peach slices instead of apricots.

## ICED TEA

2 tsp tea leaves (or 2 teabags)
3 pints (1½ litres) boiling water
3 tabsps honey
ice, lemon juice, mint leaves

Make the tea in the usual manner, allowing it to infuse for 5 minutes.
Strain into a clean jug and stir in the honey. Leave to cool before chilling.
Add lemon juice to taste and serve poured over ice with a sprig of mint.

## SWEETS AND CONFECTIONERY

### BANANA AND HONEY SPREAD

1 oz (25 g) butter or margarine
2 bananas
1 tbsp (15 ml) honey

Mix butter and honey, add mashed banana and mix well. Spread on bread or
toast (enough for 4 buttered slices).

The following recipes refer to 'hard ball', 'soft ball' etc. If you do not have a
sugar thermometer add one drop of the mixture to a cup of cold water to test.

### TURKISH DELIGHT

1 lb (450 g) granulated sugar
1½ pints (750 ml) water
2 oz (50 g) honey
7 oz (175 g) icing sugar
3 oz (75 g) cornflour
¼ level tsp cream of tartar
pink colouring
a few drops of rosewater or lemon juice
extra icing for dredging
a greased tin 7″ × 7″ (18 cm × 18 cm)

Put granulated sugar and ¼ pint water in a pan and heat to soft ball stage (120°C (240°F)). Remove from heat and add cream of tartar. Mix cornflour and icing sugar with a little of remaining water. Boil the rest of the water and pour on to the cornflour mixture, stirring until smooth. Return it to the pan, bring to the boil, stirring well, until clear and thick. Add syrup gradually, still stirring vigorously. Boil 20–30 minutes until pale yellow and transparent. Add honey and flavourings. Stir well.

Put half the mixture in tin. Add colouring to other half and pour over. When cold, cut into squares with knife dipped in icing sugar.

Toss pieces in icing sugar. Next day, store in box or tin with lid.

## HONEY FRUIT FUDGE

1 lb (450 g) sugar
4 oz (100 g) honey
2 egg whites
¼ pint (125 ml) water
¼ level tsp cream of tartar
4 oz fruit (glace cherries, angelica, almonds—optional)

Grease tin, 7″ × 7″ (18 cm × 18 cm). Put sugar, honey and water into thick bottomed pan. Warm until dissolved. Heat until hard ball stage (135°C (265°F)). Whisk egg whites until stiff and pour boiling syrup on to them. Continue whisking until it is thick and no longer glossy.

Pour into tin. Leave about 12 hours. Cut into squares with knife dipped in hot water. Fruit and nuts may be added at the end, before pouring into the tin.

## CHOCOLATE FUDGE

1 lb (450 g) granulated sugar
2 oz (50 g) honey
4 oz (100 g) plain chocolate
¼ pint (125 ml) milk
5 oz (125 g) butter or margarine
greased tin, 7″ × 7″ (18 cm × 18 cm)

Put all ingredients in a thick bottomed pan. Stir over a low heat until sugar is dissolved. Bring to the boil and heat to the soft ball stage (120°C (240° F)). Remove from heat. Stand pan in cold water for a few minutes, then beat with a wooden spoon until thick and creamy.

Pour into tin. Mark into squares and cut along marks when cool.

# NOUGAT DE MONTELIMAR

rice paper
3 oz (75 g) honey
1 pint (500 ml) water
2 oz (50 g) glace cherries
12 oz (300 g) sugar
1 oz (25 g) angelica
4 oz (100 g) toasted almonds
3 egg whites
2 oz (50 g) powdered glucose
a few drops of vanilla essence
tin, 7" × 5" (18 cm × 13 cm)

Damp the tin and line with rice paper. Melt the honey in a basin over hot water. Add the stiffly beaten egg whites. Beat until thick. Chop cherries, angelica and almonds. Mix together.

Dissolve the sugar in water in a thick bottomed pan. Add glucose and boil to 135°C (266°F) (soft crack stage). Add vanilla essence. Pour this syrup onto honey mixture and continue beating over hot water until a little of the mixture forms a hard ball when dropped into cold water, approximately 30 minutes. Add fruit and nuts. Pour into tin. Cover with rice paper. Put a weight on top. Leave until cold. Cut into squares and wrap in greaseproof or waxed paper.


# ALMOND TOFFEE

1 lb (450 g) Demerara Sugar
1 oz (50 g) butter or margarine
½ tsp vinegar
¼ pint (125 ml) water
½ level tsp cream of tartar
2 level tbsp (30 ml) honey
3 oz (75 g) chopped almonds
greased tin, 7" × 7" (18 cm × 18 cm)

Using a thick bottomed pan, with a lid, put in sugar and water. Dissolve and bring to the boil. Add butter, cream of tartar, vinegar and honey. Stir until well mixed. Replace lid. Bring to the boil. Remove the lid and heat to hard crack stage 150°C (300°F). Pour into tin. Sprinkle nuts on top. Cut into squares when nearly set. Wrap in greaseproof paper and store in airtight tin.

## HONEY FUDGE (without eggs)

1 lb (450 g) granulated sugar
¼ pint (125 ml) evaporated milk
2½ oz (60 g) butter or margarine
3 tbsp (45 ml) honey
a pinch of cream of tartar

Put all the ingredients into a pan over a low heat, stirring all the time until a little of the mixture dropped into cold water will form a 'soft ball'. Stand the pan in cold water for 5 minutes. Remove pan and beat the mixture until it begins to thicken. Pour quickly into a greased tin. When cool mark into squares.


## HONEY TOFFEE

12 oz (350 g) sugar
1 oz (25 g) butter
2½ fl oz (60 ml) water
3 oz (75 g) honey
1 dsp (10 ml) golden syrup

Melt the sugar, syrup and water in a pan on a low heat. Boil, stirring all the time until a little dropped in cold water forms a soft ball. Add the butter and honey and boil, still stirring until a drop is brittle when put in cold water. Pour into a greased tin and mark into squares before it becomes too brittle.


## PEANUT HONEY SAUCE (for ice cream)

½ lb (225 g) peanut butter
½ pint (250 ml) double cream
6 oz (150 g) soft brown sugar
1 heaped tabsp honey

Combine all the ingredients and heat gently in a saucepan or microwave, stirring frequently, until all is melted and mixed together. Raise the heat and simmer for about 5 minutes still stirring frequently. Keep warm until ready to pour over ice cream. Any unused sauce can be stored in a refrigerator for a few days and warmed gently before use.

# BEESWAX AND OTHER BEE PRODUCTS

**WAX POLISH** (To clean and shine furniture etc)

4 oz (100 g) beeswax
1 pint (500 ml) genuine turpentine
1 oz (25 g) pure soap flakes
2 tbsp (30 ml) white vinegar
¼ pint (125 ml) rainwater

*Equipment*
a jug or similar shaped vessel that will hold 2 pints (plastic
    is suitable)
a wooden spoon or spatula
a saucepan large enough to take the jug
a trivet on which to stand the jug
a bowl to mix the soap flakes

Measure the turpentine into the jug. Break the beeswax into several pieces
and add to the turpentine. Leave covered in a warm place for about 24 hours
for the wax to soften.

Stand the trivet in the pan, stand the jug on it and add water in the pan to
come well up the sides of the jug. Warm the water, keeping well under
boiling point until the wax is melted.

In another pan put the rainwater (or soft water) and add the soap flakes.
Stir until well dissolved then add the vinegar and mix well. While still warm
add to the turps and wax and stir well. Turn off the heat and leave to cool,
stirring frequently. When cool, pour into jars with well fitting lids. Apply to
furniture with a soft cloth, rub well then polish with a soft, clean duster.

## BEESWAX FURNITURE POLISH

2 oz (50 g) beeswax
2 oz (50 g) white wax (candle ends)
4 oz (100 g) soap flakes or castile soap
1 pint (500 ml) genuine turpentine

Grate the soap (if using castile) and break the wax into small pieces. Melt in a
jug or basin in a pan of hot water on the cooker. When liquid remove from
the hob and beat in the turps. When well mixed pour into jars or tins. Put to
cool and harden then cover with airtight lids.

## BEESWAX SHOE POLISH

1 ½ (37 g) clean beeswax
2 ½ fl oz (60 ml) genuine turpentine

Melt the wax into the turpentine in a container standing in hot water, or leave in a warm place, covered until melted.

*For clear polish* take a teaspoon (5 ml) of the wax paste and add 1 teaspoon (5 ml) of raw linseed oil. Stir well. Add this to the paste in the container, stirring it in well. Store in airtight jars or tins with lids.

*For black and brown polish* add black or brown oil paint with the linseed. Mix well and store as above.

## WATERPROOFING FOR LEATHER SHOES

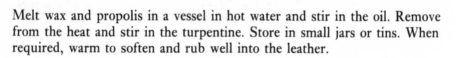

4 oz (100 g) beeswax
4 oz (100 g) propolis
1 pint (500 ml) linseed oil
¼ pint (125 ml) turpentine

Melt wax and propolis in a vessel in hot water and stir in the oil. Remove from the heat and stir in the turpentine. Store in small jars or tins. When required, warm to soften and rub well into the leather.

## USING BEESWAX IN THE HOME

Rub a piece of beeswax into the thread of wood screws which will make them easier to screw in and out again without having rusted years later.

Nails, stabbed into a piece of beeswax will drive in easily.

Rub the teeth of a saw with beeswax to prevent it binding when sawing green wood.

## PROPOLIS CORN CURE

Soften a piece of clean propolis in the fingers, spread it on a piece of thin soft leather and bind on to the corn, which will drop out in 1–2 weeks!

## TO FILL SMALL HOLES IN FURNITURE

Put equal quantities of beeswax and propolis in a jar. Stand on a trivet in a pan of hot water and warm until amalgamated. While still soft fill the holes. Smooth over with fine sandpaper.

# HONEY COUGH SYRUP

Boil a lemon slowly for 10 minutes until softened. Cut it and squeeze out the juice. To the juice add 2 tbsp (30 ml) of glycerine. Mix well then stir in 4 oz (100 g) of honey. Mix well. Take 1 teaspoon (5 ml) as required.

# ROOTING PLANT CUTTINGS

Stir a tsp (5 ml) honey into 10 fl oz (250 ml) water with a few crystals of permanganate of potash. Stand the cuttings in this solution for about 1 hour before planting.

# MEAD

The best meads are made from honey chosen for its flavour, purity and quality. Dry mead is best made with a light honey, while dark honey will make a more robust mead. Clover, apple and lime honey will make a good dry mead, blackberry hawthorn, dandelion and heather honeys are good for sweet mead. Rape is not generally accepted as having a good flavour for mead, but is improved by combining it with a stronger flavoured honey.

Many beekeepers wash and strain their cappings for mead making, but if doing this the solution should be sulphited with a campden tablet to kill any wild yeasts that may be present.

Honey has a low acid content so citric acid is usually added.

The trace elements of yeast nutrient are usually small, so it is essential to add some nutrient. It is also deficient in tannin, so a small amount of grape tannin will improve the flavour.

Honey contains some wild yeasts that may spoil the flavour, so use a mead or all purpose yeast. It is important that all the equipment used is sterilised.

A *YEAST STARTER* should be made first

**4 fl oz (100 ml) fresh orange juice**
**2 level tsp (10 ml) sugar**
**mead or all purpose yeast**

Sterilise a small jar or bottle with sulphite solution or by boiling it. Plug the mouth of the jar with cotton wool. In a small pan heat the orange juice and sugar to boiling point. Cover and leave to cool to 21°C (70°F) transfer to the sterilised bottle, add the yeast, re-insert the plug and leave in a warm place for two or three days, by which it should have started fermenting.

## DRY MEAD

3–3½ lbs (1.5 kg) light honey
1 gallon (4.5 ltr) water
1 rounded tsp (10 ml) grape tannin
½ oz (15 g) citric acid
1 level tsp (5 ml) yeast nutrient

Mix the honey and water in a pan and heat to 65°C (150°F).
Remove all the scum that comes to the surface. Add the tannin,
acid and yeast nutrient and cover to prevent dust settling. Leave it
to cool to 21°C (70°F). Add the active yeast culture and stir in well. Pour into a
sterilised 1 gallon demi-john but fill it only three quarters full. Pour the
remainder into a second jar and fit an airlock to both.

Ferment at 21°C (70°F) until the first vigorous fermentation slows down, then add the contents of the second jar to the first, leaving an airspace of about 1 inch (2.54 cm) between the mead and the cork. Leave it to ferment at about 18°C (65°F) until no more bubbles appear. Transfer to a fresh sterilised bottle and store in a cool place. Leave for about a month and check that it has stopped fermenting. Syphon into sterilised wine bottles with new, boiled, straight corks. Keep in a dark place at a temperature of not more than 13°C (55°F). Try to leave for at least a year before drinking.

## SWEET MEAD

4–4½ lb (1.8–2 kg) medium or dark honey
1 gallon (4.5 ltr) water
1 rounded tsp (10 ml) grape tannin
1 level tsp (5 ml) yeast nutrient
½ oz (15 g) citric acid
all purpose or mead yeast

Make in the same way as dry mead, starting with 3½ lbs of honey and half filling two demi-johns. A week later syphon off a pint of liquid from each jar and add half a pound of honey to each. Return to the demi-johns and continue to ferment at 21°C (70°F).

As fermentation slows down transfer by syphoning into a single jar. Do not disturb the sediment. Leave to ferment at 18°C (65°F) until no more bubbles appear. Transfer to a sterilised demi-john with a boiled cork, or to wine bottles with straight corks and store in a cool place for a year or more.

# SOME RECIPES FROM THE PAST

HONEY BALLS—for a tickling throat
Put into a small basin a knob of butter and blend it with a dessertspoon of granulated honey. Make into very small balls. Let one dissolve in the mouth when a cough is troublesome. (Most helpful with children.)

HONEY AND LEMON
To the strained juice of a ripe lemon add 1 dessertspoon of honey and ½ pint of boiling water. Drink very hot after getting into bed to ensure a good sleep and ward off a heavy cold.

HONEY FLY PAPER
Take 3 parts honey, 3 parts of resin, 1 part colza (rape) oil. Heat resin (in double saucepan) over slow heat. When melted stir in honey and oil. Spread on strips of paper while hot and turn paper end over triangles of wire (e.g. paper clip).

# Index of Recipes

Almond toffee  57
Apple, celery and walnut salad  51
Apple crunch  36
Apple flapjack pudding  41
Apple and honey cheesecake  37
Apple jelly  36
Apple meringue pie  42
Apple sauce  21
Apricot nectar  54
Apricot sweet  38

Bacon slices  16
Banana and apricot pudding  43
Banana cream  40
Banana and honey spread  55
Banana longboat  31
Banana syllabub  39
Bananas in rum sauce  32
Baps  27
Bara Brith  27
Barbecued spare ribs  13
Beef with ginger  19
*BEESWAX AND OTHER BEE*
    *PRODUCTS*  59
  Beeswax-uses  60
  Furniture polish  59
  Plant cuttings  61
  Propolis  60
  Shoe polish  60
  Waterproofing  60
  Wax polish  59
Beetroot salad  51
Blackcurrant and peach dessert  38
Bourbon biscuits  11
Braised butter-beans and spare ribs  21
Bread  26

Carrot soup  50
Celery and apple salad  50
Chelsea buns  29
Cherry pie  42

Chicken in spicy mayonnaise  24
Chicken in tangy sauce  22
Chocolate fudge  56
Chocolate fudge sundae  34
Coconut cookies  4
Coffee rum filling  6
Crowdie  35
Cucumber salad  50

Date and ginger cake  3
Dried fruit salad  32

Fairing biscuits  10
Family cake  1
Figs with honey  33
Figs with oranges  47
Fillet steak  19
Flapjacks  8
Fruit and ginger biscuits  12
Fruit and nut tea bread  30
Fruity flapjacks  9

Gillie's honey cake  7
Ginger cake  1
Ginger and chive dressing  52
Glazed carrots  53
Glazed corned beef  18
Glazed pork chops  13
Golden crunch biscuits  12
Gooseberry fool  37
Gooseberry puree  33
Gooseberry ring  43
Grapes in honey sauce  32
Greek apricot marmalade  48
Greek style almond rolls  44
Grilled chicken  23

Hazelnut tart  46
Honey and apple tart  36
Honey apricot whips  40
Honey balls  63

Honey cake  2
Honey cough syrup  61
Honey flypaper  63
Honey fruit fudge  56
Honey fudge  58
Honey ginger biscuits  11
Honey glazed bacon and apples  15
Honey glazed ham  15
Honey pork chops  14
Honey and lemon  63
Honey lemon cream pie  41
Honey marmalade  48
Honey marmalade cake  2
Honey nut biscuits  9
Honey and oatmeal biscuits  10
Honey sponge  5
Honey tart  46
Honey teabread  4
Honey toffee  58
Horseradish sauce  21
Hot red cabbage and salad  52

Iced tea  55

Joyce's date and ginger cake  3

Lamb and apple stew  16
Lamb with lemon and honey  20
Lamb steaks  17
Lamb-stuffed breast  18
Lardy cake  29
Leg of lamb  17
Lemon snow  33

Marinated mackerel  25
Mead–dry  62
Mead–sweet  62
Milk loaf  28
Milk rolls  28
Mixed fruit brulée  44

Nougat de Montelimar  57

Oat cookies  8

Oaty fruit biscuits  9
Open cherry pie  42
Orange and honey sauce  47
Orange loaf  7

Parkin  5
Peaches with almonds  31
Peanut honey sauce  58
Pears with chocolate sauce  34
Pears with orange and chocolate sauce  30
Pheasant with cranberry stuffing  23
Plum sauce with orange  35

Raisin and oat biscuits  8
Raspberry cheesecake  45
Raspberry syllabub  39
Red cabbage and apple salad  52
Rooting cuttings  61

Sausage rolls  25
Sausages with barbecue sauce  20
Scottish cream  40
Seedy cake  5
Soft white frosting  6
Spiced apple cake  3
Spiced chicken wings  22
Spiced red cabbage  53
Strawberries with port  39
Strawberry cocktail  54
Stuffed breast of lamb  18
Sweet and sour pork balls  14

Theresa's marmalade  48
Turkish delight  55

Vegetable kebabs  54
Vegetable salad with honey dressing  52
Victorian honey chutney  49
Vietnamese style stir-fried prawns  26

Whisky and oatmeal syllabub  48
White frosting  6

Yoghurt and raspberry filling  6